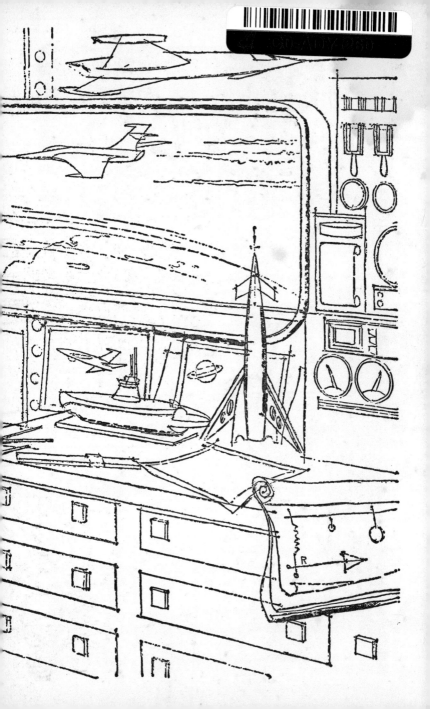

TOM SWIFT AND THE TRIPHIBIAN ATOMICAR

An atomic-powered car that travels on land, water, and through the air—Tom Swift Jr.'s latest invention—is an extraordinary achievement. But even its young inventor could not anticipate what a dramatic role the triphibian atomicar would play in a technical aid mission which takes Tom and his top-flight engineers to the untamed Asian land of Kabulistan, to help that new republic develop its natural resources.

Time and again Tom must pit his skill and courage against fierce, nomadic tribesmen. But this is not a one-sided conflict between the ancient and the modern. Beneath the façade of thunderous hoofbeats, spears, and scimitars is a scientific mastermind bent on destroying the members of the Swift expedition in order to conceal from the Kabulistan government his discovery of a fabulous ruby mine lost for two centuries.

After a series of danger-packed episodes, Tom and his pal Bud Barclay are caught in a seemingly inextricable, underground trap. How Tom builds a "do-it-yourself" rocket in a cavern laboratory and sends it homing for aid is a brilliant stroke of ingenuity.

The young scientist-inventor's daring exploits in the primitive Middle East country of Kabulistan will keep the reader breathless with suspense until the last page of this gripping story.

"Swift! Surrender or drown like rats!" their captor's voice barked over the loud-speaker

THE NEW TOM SWIFT JR. ADVENTURES

TOM SWIFT

AND HIS TRIPHIBIAN

ATOMICAR

BY VICTOR APPLETON II

ILLUSTRATED BY CHARLES BREY

NEW YORK

GROSSET & DUNLAP

PUBLISHERS

PRINTED IN THE UNITED STATES OF AMERICA

CONTENTS

CHAPTER I

AIRPORT ALARM

"TOM, your new atomic sports car is absolutely dreamy!" said Phyllis Newton.

Eighteen-year-old Tom Swift Jr. grinned at the pretty, dark-haired girl's excitement as his sleek, bronze racer glided along the highway leading out of Shopton.

"You should call it the *Silent Streak!*" suggested Sandra Swift, Tom's seventeen-year-old blond sister, who was riding in the back seat with Bud Barclay.

"Good name, Sandy," Tom agreed, "but the publicity releases will call it a triphibian atomicar."

"Open 'er up, skipper!" Bud urged his pal.

Tom advanced the unicontrol lever and the car arrowed forward with a *whoosh!* His three companions were thrilled by its smooth, noiseless response.

11

Suddenly Sandy gasped.

"Tom! Slow down for this curve!" she begged.

But instead of slowing, the bubble-hooded atomicar hurtled straight toward a stone wall.

Bud Barclay clutched the back of Tom's bucket seat. "What's wrong?" he gulped.

"Don't know!" Tom cried, frantically thumbing the brake button on top of the steering lever as he swung the lever hard left.

No response! In seconds the car would plow into the embankment like a bronze thunderbolt!

In the nick of time Tom pressed the repelatron-lifter switch on the dashboard. The atomicar zoomed up off the road—cleared the embankment with inches to spare—and finally settled down to a pancake landing in the field beyond as Tom cut off all power.

"Oh, my g-g-goodness!" Phyl quavered weakly.

Both girls were white-faced and breathless from the near accident. Tom and his husky, dark-haired pal felt a bit shaken themselves.

"Whew! Have you figured out what happened?" Bud asked when he found his voice.

"Not yet, but I intend to—pronto!"

Tom slid back the canopy, leaped out, and raised the car's hood. After a brief inspection he located the trouble.

"The master servo-control unit failed," he muttered grimly. "No wonder she wouldn't answer the stick!"

"Couldn't be sabotage, could it?" Bud asked. Often in the past, unscrupulous rivals and enemies of the Swifts had tried to wreck their new inventions or daring scientific projects.

Tom shook his head. "No sign the unit was tampered with. Even at Cape Canaveral, or our own rocket launchings on Fearing Island, there's no way to guarantee one hundred per cent reliability."

Tom took a tool kit and spare parts from the trunk, and quickly replaced the unit. He also installed an extra master control as an emergency stand-by to rule out any danger of a second mishap.

"Sorry about the scare," Tom told the girls as he and Bud climbed back into the car.

Bud chuckled. "This is what's known as getting the bugs out of a new hot rod—the hard way!"

"Please! Let's not joke about it!" said Phyl.

"Tell you what," Tom said as he steered the car in a gentle glide back onto the highway. "I'll invent an anticrash device before your next test ride, mademoiselle."

"Sold!" Phyl's brown eyes twinkled back at the young scientist.

She and Sandy soon forgot the frightening experience in the sheer exhilaration of spinning along as quietly as a breeze. The lack of engine noise, Tom explained, was due to the car being driven by four small electric motors, one of them mounted at each wheel.

"And that steering lever does everything?" Phyl asked.

"Practically everything," Tom said. "Accelerates, slows, stops, turns, or reverses—depending on how you move the stick."

Passing motorists goggled admiringly at the bronze, bubble-hooded sports car. As Tom drove farther into the country, the highway skirted pleasant green woodland on the left, while off to the right the blue waters of Lake Carlopa sparkled in the June sunshine.

"How about that *tri*phibian feature you mentioned?" Sandy asked from the back seat.

"Well, you know what *am*phibian means."

Sandy grinned at him in the rear-view mirror. "Don't pin me down, professor, but it refers to something that exists on both land and water, doesn't it? I know the Marines make amphibian landings and an amphibian plane can take off from land or water."

Tom nodded. "Well, my atomicar is *tri*phibian —meaning it can get around on land, through the air, or over water."

To demonstrate, Tom pushed the repelatron switch on the dashboard, and again the car's wheels soared gently up off the road.

"A repelatron lifter does the trick," Tom explained. The repelatron was a repulsion-ray device which Tom had invented to drive his revolutionary spaceship, the *Challenger*.

Tom brought squeals of excitement from the girls by veering off the highway, hedgehopping straight down to the shore of the lake, and then skimming out over the waves.

"Oh, this is fun!" Phyl exclaimed. "What makes the car go, now that the wheels aren't driving us?"

"A small air jet," Tom replied. "Doesn't take much motive power once we're air-borne—you could push it along with one finger."

Sandy looked down at the blue scudding surface just below them. "It's like surf-sledding!" she said gleefully. "But what if our repelatron conked out—would we float?"

"Sure." Tom flicked the switch and the car settled down on the waves with a slight splash. "Everything's watertight and there's an air ballast tank on each side of the frame."

"Great for a fishing trip!" said Bud.

"It'll be great for all sorts of transport purposes," Tom said. "This baby can cross rivers and operate over any terrain—swamps, wild bush country, even mountainous areas."

Its repelatron, the young inventor added, made the atomicar far nimbler than ground-hugging air-cushion vehicles. Moreover, it would not churn up clouds of dust on dirt roads as they do. Tom proved its versatility on the way back to town by more hedgehopping stunts—even skimming a treetop.

"Seriously, though," Tom added, as the girls caught their breaths amid gasps of laughter, "the biggest selling point is that the car will run for hundreds of thousands of miles at almost no operating cost—that is, when my new atomic power capsule is installed."

This midget power plant—a revolutionary breakthrough in itself—would change atomic energy directly into electricity. Tom explained that the present sports car model of his atomicar —for demonstration purposes—was being temporarily powered by solar batteries. The latter, another of Tom's inventions, were small powerful electric cells charged by the sun's rays at the Swifts' outpost in space. This was the Swifts' manned space installation, a wheel-shaped "factory," which they had recently assembled.

"How soon will your atomic capsule be ready to install, skipper?" Bud asked.

Tom shrugged and grinned. "I'll answer that tomorrow after we've tested it in the lab."

Sandy glanced at her wrist watch as they neared Shopton. "Gracious! This ride's been so thrilling, I almost forgot we're to meet Cousin Ed at the airport at four-fifteen!"

Tom whistled. "Good thing you reminded me!"

After dropping Phyllis Newton at her house,

the others drove on to the Swift home. Here Tom turned over the atomicar to Bud, who would drive it back to the Swifts' experimental station. Then Tom and his sister headed for the Shopton airport in the family car.

Ed Longstreet, a slender young man of twenty-five with a good-humored grin, was one of the first passengers to reach the exit gate.

"Hi, Ed! How's the world traveler these days?" Tom said, shaking his cousin's hand.

"Just great! And say! Who's this blond charmer?"

Sandy giggled and gave Ed a quick kiss.

Then they followed the stream of passengers into the terminal building. As they waited at the luggage counter, Ed described his flight home from the Middle East via London.

His remarks were interrupted as a tense voice blared out over the public-address system:

"Everyone leave the terminal at once! Repeat —leave the terminal at once! There is no cause for panic, but please get out quickly!"

There was a stunned hush, then an excited babble as people began hurrying toward the exits. Tom grabbed Sandy's hand and spoke to his cousin. "Come on, Ed! Let's go!"

The three had just reached the parking lot outside when a loud blast was heard. Smoke billowed from the airport building.

"A bomb!" Tom cried.

Fire sirens were already screaming in the distance. In a short time a hook and ladder arrived, followed by a police car, then another fire truck. The crowd watched anxiously as the police and firemen plunged into the smoking interior.

In twenty minutes exhaust fans had cleared away the last wisps of smoke, and the same voice —much calmer now—was announcing:

"Ladies and gentlemen, we regret this shocking inconvenience, but the terminal is now perfectly safe. The blast was caused by a smoke bomb, and we hope the police will soon arrest the person responsible!"

Most of the crowd showed signs of relief, although some were still angry and shaken.

"Well, well," joked Ed Longstreet, mopping his forehead with a handkerchief. "Quite a welcome you folks arranged for me!"

Tom laughed wryly and told Sandy to take their cousin to the car while he picked up Ed's suitcase. Soon the Swifts and their guest were driving home.

When they arrived, Tom's parents greeted Ed warmly. Then Mrs. Swift, slender and pretty, served glasses of iced fruit juice while their visitor settled himself in an easy chair and Sandy recounted the airport bomb scare. Mr. Swift, tall and athletic-looking, with steel-blue eyes, listened with keen interest.

"Sounds as though someone has an unpleasant

Smoke billowed from the airport building

sense of humor," he remarked quietly. The distinguished scientist and his famous son bore a close resemblance.

Ed Longstreet reached inside his suit-coat pocket and brought out a leather case which he handed to Mrs. Swift. Her eyes danced in anticipation.

Inside lay a delicate silver necklace supporting a blood-red ruby pendant. The jewel flashed with fiery brilliance as Mrs. Swift held the necklace up to the light.

"This is magnificent," she said.

"Try it on," Ed urged with a smile.

"You surely didn't bring this for me?" Mrs. Swift's voice trembled in genuine awe.

Ed nodded and produced a smaller box for Sandy. It contained a silver ring with a ruby that looked like a twin to the one in the necklace. Sandy bubbled with delight. "Oh, it's beautiful— just *beautiful!*"

Both she and her mother smiled happily as they expressed their thanks and displayed the gifts to Tom Sr. and Tom Jr. Ed was pleased.

"Actually the stones were a bargain," he explained. "I bought them unset at the bazaar in Teheran."

"That's the capital city of Iran, isn't it?" asked Sandy, more fascinated than ever.

"Yes. Persia was its old name. By the way,"

Ed went on, "there's a mystery connected with those rubies."

"A mystery!" Sandy was wide-eyed.

Ed's eyes twinkled. "No doubt you've read in the newspapers recently about Kabulistan—a little country near Iran and Afghanistan which just gained its independence. Well, once a famous ruby mine was located there, called the Amir's Mine. Today no one knows where it is—the mine's been lost for two centuries."

"You don't mean these two rubies came from that mine?" asked Tom.

"You've guessed it," said Ed. "I took the stones to London to be mounted—and because of their color, the jeweler suspected they had been taken at least two hundred years ago from the fabled lost mine of Kabulistan!"

"Oh, how fascinating!" Sandy exclaimed, and her mother added, "What a treasure trove if someone could find it!"

Ed smiled, "Believe it or not, I brought a book which gives a clue to the mine's location! I'm giving it to Tom Sr. and Tom Jr."

Going over to his suitcase, which had been placed on the stairway, Ed opened it and delved inside. His face took on a strange look as he rummaged through the contents.

"The book's gone!" he cried.

CHAPTER II

CAPSULE EXPLOSION

"ARE YOU sure you packed the book?" Tom asked his cousin.

"Positive! And it may be the only copy in existence! That book's worth a fortune if it really holds the secret of the Amir's Mine!"

Ed continued to search frantically through his suitcase, but he finally gave up in despair.

"What's the name of the book?" Sandy asked.

"*Travels in Remotest Araby*," Ed replied, "written in 1728 by an Englishman named Dalton."

Ed explained that after hearing the jeweler's chance remark, he had hunted up books of the period which told about Kabulistan. In an old bookshop in London, he had finally come upon *Travels in Remotest Araby*, which described the author's own visit to the mine.

"What a fool I was not to be more careful!" Ed chided himself. "Anyone could pick the lock of this suitcase with a safety pin! Someone must have stolen the book while I was on my way to Shopton!"

Suddenly Tom's blue eyes flashed with suspicion. "That bomb scare at the airport! It might have been arranged to give the thief a chance to rifle your suitcase at the luggage counter!"

Tom strode to the phone and dialed his friend Chief Slater at Shopton Police Headquarters. After telling the reason for his call, Tom asked for details on the bomb incident.

"Soon after the New York flight arrived, we got an anonymous phone tip that a bomb had been set to go off in the terminal," Chief Slater said. "Naturally I called the airport and ordered them to clear the building at once. No sense taking chances! Since then, we've traced the warning call to a booth right there at the terminal."

"Did anyone notice the caller?" Tom asked.

"Yes. An airline clerk gave us his description —a tall, sallow-faced man with several gold teeth, wearing a light-colored tropical suit."

Tom turned and called the description to Ed. "Why, that fellow sat right next to me!" Ed exclaimed. "He tried to draw me into conversation!"

Tom passed this information on to Chief Slater. "Good lead," the officer remarked. "We'll check the airline passenger list, although the man probably used a phony name. I'll let you know if we find him, Tom."

"Thanks, Chief." Tom hung up the phone and returned to the others with a thoughtful frown. "Looks as though you're right about that book's value, Ed. Either 'Mr. Goldtooth' wants to find that lost ruby mine himself, or he's determined to keep you from finding any clues to it."

Mrs. Swift, hoping to take their visitor's mind off his disappointing loss, hurriedly asked Sandy to help her set the table for dinner. An appetizing aroma of fried chicken and biscuits was already wafting from the kitchen.

Meanwhile, Tom and his father again examined the rubies with admiring interest. "Wonder how these would work as masers?" Tom Jr. remarked.

"*Masers?* What are those?" Ed inquired.

"Devices for generating and amplifying microwaves," Tom replied. "But I was speaking of optical masers—or lasers, as some people call them. You pump the atoms of the maser full of energy and they give off light waves of a single precise frequency, just as an oscillator in a radio emits one frequency."

With a maser made from a ruby rod, Tom went on, it was possible to generate a powerful concentrated light beam with the waves all in precise phase.

"Why not use an ordinary spotlight?" Ed asked.

Mr. Swift smiled. "By comparison, that would be pretty crude—like a radio signal sent from an electric spark. A ruby maser gives a beam of only one frequency."

"It makes an ideal method of communication," Tom added, "because a light beam, being of much higher frequency, can carry far more information than a radio channel. For instance, a maser signal of 100,000 megacycles can carry as much information as all the radio communication channels now in existence."

Ed looked impressed. "Really efficient, eh?"

"Yes, I've been experimenting with it as a method of space communication up at the outpost," Tom told his guest. "Could come in handy if an enemy ever jammed our radio signals. Of course, I've been using pink synthetic rubies. These natural ones contain more chromium atoms. It would be interesting to see what kind of maser action these produce."

"Well, don't think you're going to experiment with my ring before I even wear it!" Sandy called.

Over dinner, Ed Longstreet held the Swifts enthralled as he told about the countries he had visited in the Middle East.

"Did you go to Kabulistan?" Sandy asked.

"No, I couldn't get a plane reservation," Ed said regretfully. "Now that the country's been opened up to the outside world, so many foreign tourists and businessmen are flocking in that the few scheduled flights are sold out far in advance."

Ed threw a glance at Tom. "Speaking of businessmen, I met a banker named Provard who was very much interested to hear that I was related to the famous Swift inventors."

"An American?" Tom asked.

"Yes. I got the impression Mr. Provard might get in touch with you."

"Maybe he wants Tom to invent a new burglar alarm for his bank vault." Sandy giggled.

"More likely he's checking up on our credit," Tom said dryly. "Dad, you'd better make sure my atomic power capsule experiments aren't putting us in the red."

Mr. Swift laughed. "No danger yet, son. I have an idea the capsule could be the most profitable project Swift Enterprises has ever undertaken!"

In the morning, while Mr. and Mrs. Swift and Sandy prepared for a day's sail with their guest and Phyl Newton's family aboard the beautiful ketch *Sunspot,* Tom sped off to his private lab at Swift Enterprises. This sprawling, four-square-mile enclosure of gleaming modern workshops and laboratories was the experimental station where Tom Jr. and Tom Sr. developed their scientific marvels.

Tom was eager to run the final tests on his new midget power plant. Now that his atomicar was ready for public presentation, the only step re-

maining was to install the atomic power capsule
—provided it checked out satisfactorily.

"A big *if!*" Tom thought wryly.

A steel-and-concrete booth, radiation-shielded
by Mr. Swift's amazing plastic, called Tomasite,
had been built in one corner of the laboratory.
A special exhaust system was provided to dispose
of dangerous atomic vapors. The booth also had
a quartz-glass window and outside control panel.
Inside, mounted on a test stand, lay the power
capsule—about the size of an ordinary automo-
bile battery but far lighter in weight.

Tom was just completing the electrical hookup
when an alarm bell clanged. He jerked to attention. "The main radar alarm!"

Flicking on the radarscope, he saw a blip of
light moving in a rapid curve about the center of
the screen—evidently an aircraft!

Tom snatched up the wall phone and dialed
the control tower. "What's going on out there?"

"A small jet's circling the plant," the tower
operator reported. "The pilot requests permis-
sion to land. Says his name is Simon Wayne."

"What's his business?" Tom asked.

"He claims he wants to see you personally on
an important matter."

Tom hesitated. "Okay. Set him down."

Tom left his glass-walled lab and went outside.
He shaded his eyes as he looked skyward. A sleek
jet, bearing a red-and-black insigne, came whis-

tling down onto one of the concrete runways. Tom hopped into a jeep and sped out to meet it.

Another jeep from the Enterprises Security Building joined Tom as he reached the station airfield. Its driver was slim, dark-haired Harlan Ames, security chief of Swift Enterprises. Ames leaped out of his jeep and stood beside Tom as he waited to greet their visitor.

The pilot of the jet proved to be a huge, ruddy-cheeked man of about forty. But even more imposing than his size was an enormous blond handlebar mustache which stuck out on either side of his bluff, weather-beaten face.

"Tom Swift?" he boomed.

Tom nodded and shook hands. "This is Harlan Ames, head of our security staff," he added.

The visitor shook hands with Ames. "I'm Simon Wayne," he explained, "American representative of Europa Fabrik—as you probably guessed from the trademark on my plane."

Europa Fabrik was well known, at least by name, to both Tom and Ames. It was a European firm, belonging to one of the biggest industrial cartels in the world.

"Rather an informal way to drop in, wasn't it?" said Ames.

Wayne's eyes froze on Ames, then he burst into a deep chuckle. "When I do things, I do 'em in a hurry!" Wayne said. "Only way to meet business competition these days. I wanted to see Tom

Swift and happened to be flying this way, so here I am!"

"What did you want to see me about?" Tom broke in politely.

Wayne abruptly turned serious. "Where can we talk business?"

Minutes later, Tom faced his visitor across a huge modern desk in the big sunlit double office which he shared with Mr. Swift.

"I'm listening, Mr. Wayne."

"I've been reading in scientific journals about your new miniature power plant which produces electrical energy directly from atomic reaction," Wayne began. "Europa Fabrik can use that process. We can use you, too. Name your price." He took out a checkbook and poised a fountain pen over it.

Tom grinned. "I'm flattered, Mr. Wayne, but the rights to my midget power plant are not for sale. Nor am I looking for a job. If you'll pardon me, my dad and I think we have the finest scientific setup in the world right here."

Wayne named a huge figure, then doubled it. Tom shook his head. "Sorry, but my answer remains No."

Wayne laughed. "Very well. I like a young fellow who knows his own mind." He replaced his checkbook and pen, then took a card from his wallet and handed it to Tom. "But if you should change your mind, the offer's still open."

After seeing his visitor take off, Tom went back to his private lab, feeling a trifle dazed from Wayne's whirlwind tactics.

"Who was Handlebar Hank?" inquired Bud, walking into the laboratory a few moments afterward.

"Fellow named Wayne from Europa Fabrik." Tom grinned as he related his visitor's offer. "But never mind him. I want to see how the Mighty Midget, here, pans out."

Bud watched eagerly from the doorway of the test booth as Tom tightened a cable connection and inspected a few final details.

The power plant was housed in a small, rectangular, capsulelike casing. It had a copper boss at each end, one positive and one negative, through which the electrical output would be drawn off. A sheathed cable led from the capsule to a small control box, which was connected to an outside control panel.

"Keep your fingers crossed, pal," the young inventor muttered as he emerged from the booth and latched the door with the twirl of a lever.

Bud, a young flier from San Francisco, and the same age as Tom, had watched the development of all his chum's major inventions, and shared many adventures as Tom's copilot. He never failed to feel a thrill when Tom tested some new brain child.

"Good luck, genius boy!"

Tom handed him dark goggles, donned a pair himself, then threw a switch.

The needle of the output wattmeter swung sharply to the right. The next moment both boys were hurled off their feet as the entire laboratory shook from a terrific blast!

CHAPTER III

AROUSED SUSPICIONS

A DISASTER siren wailed across the experimental station, as an orange-red inferno glowed behind the quartz window of the test booth.

Slowly Tom and Bud sat up, struggled to their feet, and eyed the wreckage in the laboratory with dismay. Books, file cabinets, electronic gear, and other valuable equipment lay tumbled about the floor, amid the shattered glass from fallen racks of test tubes. Smashed bottles of chemicals sent reeking fumes through the lab.

"Good grief! What happened?" Bud gasped.

"The atomic power capsule exploded—generated too much pressure and blew up," Tom said grimly.

Though dazed and bruised from their fall, neither boy was injured. Already shouts could be heard outside the laboratory as plant employees rushed to investigate the explosion.

"Bud, tell everyone to keep out!" Tom yelled.

As Bud hurried to comply, Tom glanced quickly at a radiation-level indicator. "Thank heavens!" he muttered. Evidently the reaction products had been safely confined within the test booth.

Tom snatched up the telephone and dialed Ames at Security. "Bud and I are okay," he reported, "but an atomic reaction got out of hand. Get the decontamination squad here pronto!"

The next few hours were spent in harried efforts to cope with the disaster. Tom finally organized a procedure to draw off the radioactive residue safely from the booth after the reaction had cooled. This would take several days. Then the booth itself would have to be dismantled and construction materials carefully disposed of.

It was late afternoon when Tom finally slumped into a chair in his office to relax over a pot of hot cocoa with Bud.

"Tough luck, skipper," Bud sympathized. "Did you expect this might happen?"

Tom shrugged. "I knew the risk was there. But I thought I had the pressure problem licked. I used the strongest suitable metal I could find for the capsule casing—the Lunite alloy we discovered on the phantom satellite."

"And still the capsule blew up."

"Right," Tom said gloomily. "Hang it all, Bud, I'm afraid there *is* no metal that's strong enough and yet light enough to contain my power-plant reaction process."

"Don't worry, you'll lick it yet!" Bud said, patting his pal on the shoulder. "Bet you have a new schedule of experiments all figured out."

Tom plowed his fingers through his crew cut and grinned ruefully. "Wish I did. This means our atomicar announcement will have to be postponed, and I won't even be able to use the special lab for the next few days."

The young inventor was not deterred from work by the accident. He decided, for the balance of the afternoon, to use one of the smaller labs and try some further communications experimenting with his zircon-arc powered ruby maser.

"Want to watch?" he invited Bud.

"Sure. I haven't seen this gadget of yours yet."

The boys entered the lab, and Bud took a close look at his friend's device.

"Hmm, looks like a fancy searchlight—set on an oversized pistol. Okay, Prof. Give me a breakdown of what's what."

Tom grinned and pointed to the larger end of the cone-shaped metal contrivance's housing. "Inside this part is a powering light reflector, flash lamp, and condenser for the powering light." Tom's finger moved to the narrowed "neck" of the device. "In here is the ruby rod itself."

The smaller end of the maser contained the focusing output lenses.

"And what are these for?" Bud inquired, pointing to two flexible tubes leading into the ruby-rod section.

"They're for cooling the rod—which is silvered at both ends—by a flow of fluid through them. This third tube powers the flash lamp."

"And what's this part that reminds me of a gun trigger?"

"It's a hand mount. And the 'trigger' here is the switch for turning on the power."

On top of the ruby-rod section was a control for focusing, and underneath the base of the maser was a mount for tripod operation.

"I'll try sending a message to the outpost," Tom said.

"Shoot!" Bud urged eagerly.

Tom plugged in a small throat microphone and aimed the unit directly overhead.

"I hope to make this model one hundred per cent portable soon, so we can communicate with the space station at any time," he explained.

The brief message Tom flashed took only a couple of seconds. There was a few minutes' wait. Finally, over the receiver, came the response:

"Got your message, skipper. Not very clear, but I'd say that maser could really save the day, if necessary. Over."

"Just testing, this time," Tom signaled back. "I'll be in touch with you."

After he had signed off, Bud, greatly intrigued,

said, "Wonder if you could reach any other beings in space?"

"Let's find out." Tom beamed a signal, but several attempts brought no response.

Bud grinned. "Maybe if you weren't such a cheap skate and used real rubies, you'd have better luck!"

"I agree," said Tom. "If you see any unused ones lying around, pal, let me know."

That evening, after the others had returned from the cruise, Tom brought them up to date on the day's events. Then he said, "Dad, I've just been reading some reports from the Citadel. I'm pretty sure they've given me a new lead on a casing for my midget power plant." The Citadel was the Swifts' atomic research plant in New Mexico.

As Mr. Swift listened with interest, Tom explained that he was impressed by the data on a stable isotope of one of the new man-made elements. Its physical and chemical properties sounded as though the isotope might be promising in developing a new covering for his atomic power capsule.

"In fact, I think I'll fly out to the Citadel and work on it in the lab there for a few days," Tom said.

"Oh! What a super idea!" Sandy burst out when she heard the plan. "Bud will be going, I suppose, and school's over, so why don't Phyl and I go too? And naturally you'll come along, Cousin Ed!"

Tom agreed with a smile, but Ed Longstreet declined. "It may sound silly," he said, "but I think I'll hop back to New York for a day or so. I'd like to see what I can dig up at the public library there on that lost ruby mine in Kabulistan."

Sandy darted to the telephone to call Phyllis Newton. Phyl's father was not related to the Swifts but was always called "Uncle Ned" by Tom and Sandy. Mr. Newton, Mr. Swift's old comrade-in-arms, was now manager of the Swift Construction Company, which manufactured the Swifts' inventions.

Phyl was enthusiastic over Sandy's idea and quickly obtained her parents' consent. The next day at noon, the four young people watched as the *Sky Queen* was hoisted from its underground hangar at Swift Enterprises and hauled by tractor to its special runway. This huge atomic-powered plane, often called the Flying Lab, had carried Tom on his first adventure when he found himself pitted against a band of South American rebels seeking valuable radioactive ore deposits. Recently, he had invented the electronic hydro-lung, using it to search the ocean depths to recover a Jupiter probe missile lost in the South Atlantic.

As Tom checked certain equipment aboard, a foghorn voice suddenly rattled his eardrums.

"Brand my apple dumplin's, you ain't headin' West without me, are you, boss?" Chow Winkler, the genial cook on all Swift expeditions, came stalking out on the airfield, dragging a cartful of groceries behind him.

The former chuck-wagon cook from the Texas Panhandle had first met the Swifts on one of their research trips to New Mexico. As usual, the roly-poly chef was decked out in a ten-gallon hat and gaudy sport shirt.

"Hey! Look out!" Bud warned the girls loudly, eying Chow's flame-colored shirt with a fearful expression. "I thought we had that atomic explosion all caged up!"

"You're jest jealous, Buddy boy," Chow snapped, as Sandy and Phyl laughed. Turning to Tom, he added, "Well, how about it, boss? Am I comin'?"

"Sure you're coming, old-timer," Tom said soothingly, throwing his arm around the old Texan. "We planned this trip on such short notice, I forgot to let you know."

In five minutes the *Sky Queen* roared off the runway. Streaking westward at transonic speed, the sleek, swept-wing, three-deck craft reached New Mexico in an hour.

As the painted canyons and mesas flattened into barren scrubland, the Citadel came into sight below—a pinwheel formation of ultramodern laboratory buildings and dormitories. They were grouped around a massive central dome of white concrete which housed the main reactor. The whole research plant was ringed with barbed wire and guarded by drone planes and radar.

As soon as they landed, Tom buried himself in his private laboratory. He was still deep in work the following afternoon. Bud and the two girls, knowing it was useless to disturb him, drove off in a jeep for a picnic at one of their favorite spots.

Suddenly Bud braked the jeep to a halt on the sandy trail. "Hey, what's that joker doing up there?" he muttered suspiciously.

On the mesa just above them, a figure was seated at an easel, peering through binoculars.

"Looks like an artist," said Phyl.

"Then why is he snooping at the Citadel through those glasses?" Bud demanded.

The glasses certainly appeared to be trained toward the atomic research plant. Bud jumped from the jeep and scrambled up the boulder-and-brush-strewn slope. The figure at the easel, a youngish, wiry-looking man with tousled, carrot-red hair, paused long enough to glance at him, then returned to his binoculars.

"What's the idea of those glasses?" Bud snapped.

"To see better," the man replied tersely.

"I'll bet you can," Bud said. "In case you don't know it, that's a top-secret research station!"

"I'm not likely to steal any secrets at this range."

The red-haired man looked Bud up and down with a grin. Then he raised the binoculars to his eyes again.

Enraged by the fellow's apparent arrogance, Bud snatched the glasses from his hand.

"Give those back, please," the stranger demanded.

"I'll give you a poke in the jaw if you don't explain what you're doing here!" Bud stormed, grabbing him by the front of his polo shirt.

The next thing Bud knew, a fist exploded in his face. The husky young pilot staggered back, then dropped the binoculars and waded in with his fists flying.

"Bud! Stop it!" Sandy commanded as she and Phyl came running up the slope. Between them, the girls managed to separate the opponents. "Bud—this is Orton Throme! He's the famous abstract painter!"

"And Mr. Throme is also a well-known war hero and jet pilot," Phyl added.

Bud stopped short, his jaw dropping open as he suddenly remembered various magazine accounts he had read about "Ort" Throme and his Marine fighter squadron.

"I—I'm sorry, Mr. Throme," he said, thrusting out his hand. "Guess I acted too fast,"

"Pretty powerful left hook you throw." The ace chuckled, shaking hands. "Can't blame you for being suspicious. I guess I shouldn't have been conning the Citadel with binoculars. Call me Ort, by the way."

"I'm Bud Barclay," Bud replied. "This is Sandy Swift and Phyllis Newton."

The introductions were cut short as Sandy gasped in dismay. "My ruby ring! It's—gone!"

The ring, a bit too large, had evidently slipped off her finger as she attempted to stop the fight. Bud's face flamed with embarrassment when he discovered the ring under his foot—the metal band badly bent.

Ort Throme suggested that the ring could be repaired by a famous jewelry designer in Taos, several miles away. Both Sandy and Phyl were delighted at the idea of visiting the famous art colony. Before the conversation ended, Ort had accepted an invitation to join their picnic.

The next day Bud and the girls persuaded Tom to take an afternoon off from his lab work and drive with them to Taos. The highway wound along the Rio Grande amid rabbit brush and wild flowers. Taos itself proved to be a quaint old Western town nestled at the base of the Sangre de Cristo Mountains. Some of the huge cottonwoods shading its dusty streets had been there since the days of Kit Carson, its most famous citizen.

Tom drove through the bustling plaza to the Indian reservation three miles distant. Taos Pueblo, built before Columbus discovered

America, rose from a plain at the foot of the smoky-blue range like a child's brown mud castle. It was rectangular and terraced, with crude wooden ladders leading from one story to the next higher one. Black-haired Indians, garbed in blankets, sat before the turquoise and red doors of their apartments.

"How fascinating!" Phyl exclaimed.

After touring the settlement, Tom drove back to the town. Here an Indian directed the visitors to the adobe studio of Benn Garth. The jeweler's eyes lighted as Sandy showed him her ring.

"I've never seen a ruby quite like this before," he said, examining the stone through a jeweler's loop. "Looks rather like the kind from Afghanistan, but this has much finer fire."

"Do you think it came from Kabulistan?" Tom asked casually.

Garth looked up at him. "Oddly enough, I do. I've seen only a few museum specimens from the Kabulistan mine, but this certainly resembles them in color."

At that moment Phyl gasped and pointed toward the window. As the others turned, they saw a dark-featured man in an Oriental turban suddenly duck out of sight!

CHAPTER IV

STARTLING PHONE CALL

BUD whirled into action and darted out the front door of the studio. He collided head-on with the man in the turban!

The jolt left Bud speechless for a moment. Recovering, he gripped the man's arm and demanded, "Why were you spying on us?"

"I beg your pardon, but I was not." The dark-featured man shook off Bud's arm. "I was merely passing the window on my way to enter the studio and happened to glance in. Now will you please allow me to get by?"

"Okay."

Bud stood aside and stared at him in baffled surprise. The stranger adjusted his white, gold-threaded turban, then walked in.

"My name is Mirza," he said. "Is Mr. Tom Swift Jr. here?"

Everyone looked at him in surprise. Tom spoke up, "I'm Tom Swift."

The man bowed and made a gesture of salaam. "I am the secretary to Mr. Nurhan Flambo, the head of Pan-Islamic Engineering Associates. Mr. Flambo is now at your atomic research station and urgently wishes to confer with you."

Mr. Flambo, the secretary explained, had flown from the Middle East via New York for the sole purpose of seeing Tom Swift. After landing in New Mexico he had taken a car directly from the airport to the Citadel. There, Mr. Flambo had learned of Tom Swift's trip to Taos and had sent Mirza to summon him back at once.

"Why didn't he come to Taos himself?" Bud demanded. Mirza merely shrugged.

Tom, too, was somewhat irritated by the high-handed demand. Evidently Flambo was accustomed to having people jump when he issued orders. On the other hand, if he had flown all the way from the Middle East, there must be an important reason and it seemed only polite to see him.

Tom frowned a moment, then said, "Sorry to break up our outing, Phyl and Sandy, but maybe I'd better go back. Bud, suppose you and the girls stay here. Mr. Mirza can drive me back."

Arriving at the Citadel, Tom found his visitor pacing back and forth in the lobby of the reception building. Flambo, a gaunt, hawk-nosed man with a trim black beard, greeted Tom with an angry glare.

"I have been waiting here for over four hours," he complained as they shook hands.

"A call or telegram that you were coming would have saved us both some inconvenience," Tom returned evenly. "I hope you have been comfortable."

Flambo snorted. "A ridiculous-looking cowboy brought me lunch—a concoction of rattlesnake meat. Naturally I was unable to touch it."

Tom repressed a grin. "Chow probably thought he was paying you an honor. He does prepare—er—unusual delicacies at times."

As he spoke, Tom looked over his visitor carefully. Flambo was dressed impeccably in a suit of shimmering gray silk. Tom's eye was caught by his ruby tie clasp.

"Perhaps we can talk more comfortably in my office," Tom said.

As they walked across the grounds toward one of Tom's lab buildings, the young inventor remarked, "I can't help admiring your tie clasp, sir. That's a Kabulistan ruby, isn't it?"

Flambo bared his white teeth in a sneer. "I fear your knowledge of rubies is not so expert as your scientific skill, my dear Mr. Swift. This happens to be a pigeon's-blood ruby—a gift from a colleague in India."

"My mistake," Tom said with a smile.

When they reached the office, adjoining a lab, Tom offered his guest a chair and sat down behind his desk. "What can I do for you, Mr. Flambo?"

"My company—Pan-Islamic Engineering Associates—is making a great contribution to the Middle East," Flambo said proudly. "We are building roads, bridges, and refineries—all with technicians from our own countries. A far better way than letting greedy outsiders get a foothold!"

Tom nodded. "I believe science knows no national boundaries. All countries have a right to share in scientific progress."

Flambo scowled. "Unfortunately some countries use their scientific leadership to impose their will on less advanced areas."

"Some do," Tom agreed coolly. "Not the United States."

Flambo shrugged impatiently. "In any case, my company could make good use of your new, small-sized, atomic dynamo. We are therefore prepared to offer any price within reason for the sole industrial rights to your invention."

Tom was startled. Then a smile spread over his face. "That's the second time in a few days I've had such an offer, Mr. Flambo. My answer to both offers is No. When and if my midget power plant is perfected, I intend to sell or lease it for use wherever it can help mankind."

Flambo's eyes blazed. "Meaning wherever you can use it as a tool for getting advantage over weaker countries!" he stormed.

The telephone rang. Tom picked it up, listened a few moments, then replaced the receiver with an amused look.

"Excuse me a minute, sir," Tom told Flambo. "Your secretary Mirza seems to be trying to get a foothold where *he* doesn't belong."

Tom hurried outside and found Chow Winkler holding Mirza tightly bound in the loop of his lariat.

"Caught the sidewinder sneakin' past my galley window—snoopin'!" the Texan reported.

Mirza was quivering, either from anger or fear, Tom could not decide which. The secretary's face looked livid as he muttered something unintelligible.

"All right, let him go, Chow. I'll take over," Tom said. He warned his prisoner, "An atomic research station is a dangerous place to go wandering around, Mirza. Don't try it again."

"Reckon you'd better keep an eye on that boss o' his, too," Chow warned. "I never did trust a critter that don't appreciate good vittles!"

Tom grinned and started back to his office. Mirza accompanied him silently. In the meantime, Flambo's temper seemed to have cooled down.

"Your answer to my offer, then, is a flat refusal?" he asked Tom.

"I'm afraid it will have to be, sir."

"Then there is no further point in my remaining here." Flambo turned and snapped an order to his secretary in what sounded like Arabic.

Tom, politely but firmly, insisted on accompanying them to their rented car. Then he watched until the guard at the gate flagged them through.

"Guess I may as well get back to work, now that I'm here," Tom thought.

Twenty minutes later he was pouring a batch of molten metal from a miniature electronic furnace into a keg. The white-hot mass was the new alloy, Lunite, with a 0.007 percentage of the stable isotope. Tom was wearing protective dark goggles and asbestalon gloves and apron.

Suddenly, as he finished pouring, Tom's ears caught a hissing, crackling noise behind him. He turned and gave a gasp of fear. His workbench was a mass of flames—which were shooting perilously close to a shelf full of flammable chemicals!

Tom pushed an alarm bell and grabbed up a fire extinguisher. Luckily he was able to douse the flames even before help arrived.

"What happened?" the chief of the fire crew asked, after making sure the danger was past.

"I'm not sure." Tom shoved up his goggles and began poking among the scorched debris. "Oh—oh! Here's the answer," he announced a moment later. "The electrical lead to my glass pyrometer rod must have shorted. There's a kink here, where the insulation probably frayed."

Tom's workbench was a mass of flames

The men left. Then Tom repaired the damaged electrical lead and went back to work. That night, when Bud, Sandy, and Phyl returned from Taos, the four young people enjoyed a snack of hamburgers and milk in the laboratory. Bud scowled suspiciously after hearing of the blaze, and asked:

"Did you say Flambo stayed in your office when you went out to rescue that sneaky secretary?"

Tom nodded.

"Then how do you know *he* wasn't responsible for that electrical short?" Bud demanded. "He could have slipped into the lab while you were gone."

Tom frowned. "It's possible. But why should he?"

Nevertheless, before going to bed that night, Tom sent a radio message to Harlan Ames at Enterprises. He asked the security chief to check on both Flambo and Pan-Islamic Engineering Associates.

Some time after midnight, Tom was aroused by the telephone jangling on his bedside table. He groped sleepily for the instrument.

"Hello? . . . Tom Swift speaking."

"This is Benn Garth in Taos," said the voice at the other end of the line. "I just surprised a thief breaking into my studio. Thought I'd better let you know right away. He was that man with the turban who came here looking for you!"

CHAPTER V

THE CURSE OF SHAITAN

"YOU mean Mirza?" Tom sat bolt upright, completely awake.

"Right. My studio is wired with a burglar alarm because of the precious stones and valuable jewelry I keep here," Garth explained. "When the alarm went off, I jumped out of bed and dashed to my workshop just in time to grab him. But he put up a nasty fight and finally escaped out the window."

"What about my sister's ruby ring?" Tom asked. "I assume she left it with you?"

"Yes, but don't worry. It's still here in my safe. In fact, he didn't take anything, so far as I can discover."

Garth added that he had called the police and they were making a thorough search for the suspect. They had also set up roadblocks in the hope of cutting off Mirza's escape.

"I called partly to warn you that the fellow is a criminal—maybe even dangerous," Garth said. "Also to find out if you had any information about him."

Tom told as much as he knew about Mirza and his employer. "When they left here this afternoon, Flambo claimed they were going to fly back to New York," Tom concluded. "Why not check with the airport at Albuquerque?"

"Good idea. I'll notify the police."

After Garth rang off, Tom lay awake for over an hour, thinking. Was it Sandy's ruby that Mirza had been after? Or had he just been tempted by the sight of valuable jewelry lying about the studio?

Mirza's first appearance at the studio window had certainly seemed furtive and suspicious. "And Garth had just been saying, at that moment, that the ruby might have come from the Kabulistan mine!" Tom recalled. "In either case, where does Mirza's employer, Flambo, fit into the picture?"

The thought of Flambo's ruby tie clasp flickered through Tom's mind as he finally dozed off.

When he told the others at breakfast about Mirza's breaking into the studio, Sandy exclaimed, "And to think it might have been my ring he was trying to steal!"

Bud lifted a forkful of bacon and eggs. "Maybe he's the Thief of Bagdad." Sandy, who was just finishing her orange juice, choked and sputtered with laughter.

Bud slapped her vigorously on the back, then turned to Tom. "Seriously, skipper, I warned you that creep and his boss were up to no good!"

"I guess you're right," Tom conceded.

Later that morning a second phone call from Taos informed Tom that Flambo had arrived on schedule in New York. "But Mirza was not with him," Garth added.

"How come?" Tom asked.

"Flambo told the police that just before taking off from Albuquerque, Mirza had informed him he was quitting his job and refused to accompany Flambo on the flight back. Apparently Flambo was angry at his employee. He stated that he knew nothing about Mirza's present whereabouts and cared less."

"That clears Flambo of suspicion—if he's telling the truth," Tom mused. "Thanks for letting me know, Mr. Garth."

"Don't mention it. And please tell your sister I'll have the new setting for her ruby ready on Monday."

Tom soon forgot about Mirza and the attempted burglary as he plunged back to work in his laboratory. A study of the new element's atomic structure had sparked a different train of thought.

"Why think in terms of a *metal* for the capsule casing?" Tom asked himself. "Judging from the chemical properties of the isotope in that report, it should be possible to construct molecules that would link together with terrific strength. Maybe I've been missing a bet!"

Tom's work was interrupted by two more calls that morning. The first was a radio message from Harlan Ames at Enterprises. The security chief reported that he had checked on both Flambo and Pan-Islamic Engineering Associates. "So far as is known, there is nothing detrimental against either the man or his company."

Near lunchtime, as Tom was "cooking" a bubbling brown mass of chemicals in a complicated hookup of retorts and glass tubing, Ed Longstreet telephoned from New York.

"Sorry if I'm interrupting a big scientific breakthrough," Ed teased, "but I thought you might be interested in this item of information I just dug up at the library."

"I sure am, if it has anything to do with those rubies," Tom said.

"Guess why the Amir's Mine was abandoned?" Ed challenged.

"I give up. Why?"

"Because an imam, or priest, decided that the mine was accursed by Shaitan," Ed reported. "Shaitan, you know, is the Moslem name for Satan. The thought of that curse scared everyone in Kabulistan so much that the mine workings

were abandoned and filled in. That was two centuries ago and no one has even dared look for it
since."

"I suppose the devil's curse would scare a lot of
people," Tom said thoughtfully. Then he told
his cousin about Flambo, Mirza, and the attempted burglary.

Ed was intrigued by the news. "Looks as
though you may be getting mixed up in this
ruby mystery yourself, Tom," he remarked.

Tom gave a dry chuckle. "I hope not. I am
right in the middle of a hot experiment."

"In that case, I'll hang up." Ed laughed. "But
keep me informed of developments."

"Right. So long, Ed, and thanks."

After working at a frenzied pace through most
of the week end, with only time out for a church
service, Tom decided on Monday to accompany
Bud and the girls to Taos to pick up Sandy's ring.
He wondered if Garth, or the police there, might
have fresh news about Mirza.

Chow, too, begged to go along. "Reckon I'll
mosey around town a bit while you buckaroos
are gettin' that ring," he said. As soon as their
station wagon arrived in town he hurried off.

"Don't buy any Indian shirts with purple-and-
orange thunderbirds on them!" Bud called.

Chow turned to give a dignified sniff. He had
hardly taken two steps forward again when a
plump woman with orange-yellow hair and jan-

gling silver earrings pounced on him with a glad cry. She wore a paint-smeared artist's smock.

"O-oh! What a colorful character!" she shrilled in a piercing voice. "A perfect old Western type! Such rugged, sun-bronzed features!"

"Huh?" Chow gulped. "Beg pardon, ma'am?"

His remark sent her into fresh gales of excitement. "You positively *must* pose for a painting!" she declared. "Naturally I'll pay you the top model's fee!"

Chow's face took on a pleased smirk as he realized that she was an artist and wished to paint his portrait.

"Reckon it's natural to want the real thing if you're lookin' fer a rugged, straight-shootin' cowboy," he said, doffing his ten-gallon hat. "I don't mind posin' fer a spell."

Sandy and Phyl giggled as the woman dragged him off triumphantly. The girls saw them enter a low adobe house halfway down the street.

"I think that was Lady Thunderbird herself," Bud confided in a low voice. "Come on! Let's get Sandy's ring."

Benn Garth greeted Tom and his companions at his studio and produced the new ring he had fashioned for Sandy's ruby. Bud gave a whistle of admiration and both girls gasped with delight.

"It's beautiful!" Sandy declared. "A perfect fit, too!"

The band was formed in the shape of two twining serpents, their heads and tails forming the setting for the stone.

"It's certainly a fine piece of craftsmanship," Tom remarked.

Garth invited them to have refreshments at his studio and Tom took the opportunity to inquire about Mirza.

"The police have no fresh clues," Garth said. "The funny thing is, where could he have gone in the wide-open country around here? Of course he may still be hiding in Taos. Actually there's no easy way to identify him without his turban. And the town's always thronging with tourists at this time of year."

"Are you sure the burglar *was* Mirza?" Phyl put in.

Garth frowned thoughtfully. "It's true I couldn't see his face in the darkness very well. But the burglar *did* have on a turban—and I've never seen anyone else around here wearing one."

Presently the four young people took their leave, and strolled along the pleasant streets. After bargaining with an Indian for a turquoise bracelet, Sandy said, "I wonder how Chow is getting along with Lady Thunderbird."

"We can see for ourselves," Phyl replied mischievously, pointing to the artist's house. "He's in there, probably posing for Custer's Last Stand."

As they passed the driveway beside the house,

Sandy glanced into the back yard and clapped a hand over her mouth. "Oh, no!" she exclaimed.

The others followed her to the yard, then grinned as they watched the scene before them. Seated before an easel was the stout lady artist. She wore a pleased expression. Her subject was not so happy.

Chow's leathery face bore a scowl. He wore a gaudy silk neckerchief and bearskin chaps as he posed beside a cow.

"Now pick up that branding iron," the artist ordered, "and pretend you're branding the bull."

"You don't brand 'em standin' up!" Chow protested. "An' besides, this ain't no bull."

As if in total agreement, the cow turned her head and licked Chow's face. "Get away!" the cowboy stormed.

Unable to restrain themselves any longer, Tom, Bud, and the girls burst into gales of laughter. Chow's neck reddened with embarrassment. "Sorry, ma'am," he apologized, doffing his big hat, "but I ain't no model."

Looking straight ahead, the flustered cowboy stomped out of the yard. Tom clamped a hand on his shoulder.

"Come on, old-timer. What you need is a good, juicy, three-inch steak!"

Chow brightened. "Now you're talkin', boss. An' loaded with ketchup, too!"

Darkness had fallen when the group finally

"You don't brand 'em standin' up!" Chow protested

started back to the Citadel, with Tom at the wheel. Sandy and Phyl were still chatting excitedly about the day's sightseeing. The highway was almost deserted, except for a car several hundred yards behind them.

About ten miles from Taos, the station wagon's engine suddenly began sputtering and coughing. "Wonder what's wrong," Tom said.

"Frankly, pal, it sounds as if we're out of gas," Bud said cheerfully.

"We can't be. Look at the gauge needle."

A moment later the engine died abruptly. Tom barely managed to steer off the road before the station wagon rolled to a halt. Both boys got out to check the tank and lift the hood.

The car behind now overtook them and pulled off the road just ahead of the station wagon. A bareheaded man leaped from the car, brandishing a revolver.

"Get your hands up, all of you!" he snarled in a voice that had a familiar foreign accent.

It was Mirza!

CHAPTER VI

CRUCIAL PRESSURE TEST

AS HE strode toward Tom and Bud, Mirza's face was starkly revealed in the glare of the station wagon's headlights. He looked pale and unshaven. His eyes gleamed fanatically.

Moving past the two boys, Mirza jerked open the rear door. "You three, step outside!"

Chow climbed from the back seat, scowling. Sandy and Phyl followed.

"I suppose you drained our tank while we were having dinner back in Taos," Tom accused Mirza. "And then doctored the fuel gauge."

"Most clever of you to guess," the man sneered. He turned to Sandy and held out his free hand. "I will take that ruby ring, please!"

As Sandy stepped back defiantly, Tom snapped, "I wouldn't touch that ring if I were you!"

Mirza froze. "And why not?"

"In case you've forgotten, the rubies from that lost mine in Kabulistan bear the curse of Shaitan!"

Tom's words were a mere shot in the dark. But the effect was startling. The former secretary's face contorted in fear.

"What does a young American fool like you know about the curse of Shaitan?" he blustered.

"I know that it's already bringing *you* bad luck," Tom said smoothly. "Every word we're saying is being picked up—which means a State Police car is probably on its way here right now!"

"*What!*"

"Take a look for yourself at that short-wave radio on the dashboard," Tom prodded. "It's on."

Mirza took the bait. As he bent forward slightly to glance into the station wagon, Chow's gnarled fist shot out in a whirling uppercut!

The punch caught Mirza on his outthrust chin. He tottered backward and Bud dived at his legs in a tackle that brought the man crashing to the ground. Before Mirza could bring his revolver into play, Tom wrested the gun from his hand.

"Don't try any stunts!" Tom warned.

Mirza struggled like a madman, but Bud and Chow pinned him relentlessly to the ground. Tom quickly got a length of rope from the station wagon, and Mirza was finally subdued and bound.

"Brand my tumbleweed salad!" Chow panted,

when it was all over. "The critter's plumb loco!"

Mirza gasped out a torrent of abuse in Arabic. Several times his listeners caught the word "Shaitan." Sandy and Phyl huddled together in the rear of the car, while Bud and Chow guarded the prisoner and Tom summoned help over the radio.

"Wasn't the two-way radio on?" Sandy asked.

Tom grinned. "Yes. Just in case of trouble, I turned it on when the car began to act up."

Soon a State Police car arrived. The sergeant in charge tried to question Mirza, but the prisoner gave only raving, disconnected replies.

"Beware! The ruby must be returned to Kabulistan, or hurled into the depths of the sea!" he stormed. "If not, the curse of Shaitan and his Afrites will fall upon you!"

"I guess that's all we're likely to get out of Mirza," Tom murmured.

The sergeant agreed in disgust. "I'd say this guy belongs in a padded cell."

After Tom put some gasoline into the station wagon's tank from the police car's emergency supply, he and his companions continued on to the Citadel. Meanwhile, the police headed back to Taos with their prisoner.

"Tom, do you suppose Mirza *really* believes in that curse?" Phyl asked a few moments later. "Or was the whole thing just an act?"

"If that business about the curse was just an act, he deserves an Oscar!" Sandy shuddered.

"If you ask me, he was just covering up to keep from answering questions," Bud said flatly.

Tom agreed. "For all we know, he may *still* be working for Flambo!"

The next morning Sandy, Phyl, and Bud gathered in Tom's laboratory. They watched quietly as he prepared to test the new material he had developed for his midget power-plant casing. The young inventor had extruded several rods which he now installed in a strength-testing machine.

"Did you say it's a *plastic?*" Phyl asked in amazement.

"Technically, yes," Tom replied. "But in all its properties, the material is more like a tremendously strong, hard, lightweight metal."

When the rods were installed, Tom flipped a lever. He watched the gauge needle creep slowly around its dial as hydraulic pressure built up inside the machine. Soon the sample rods were being subjected to enormous stress. One was being pulled at each end to test its tensile strength. Another was being compressed under crushing pressure. Still another was being bent, while a fourth was being twisted.

"I don't see much happening," said Sandy in a puzzled voice.

Tom grinned. "Neither do I—and that's good. It means the stuff is as strong as I had hoped."

His jubilation increased as the torture tests

continued. When the rods were removed from the machine and measured, they showed only a small amount of deformation!

"Boy! Looks as if you really have something here, skipper!" said Bud excitedly. "Have you named the stuff as yet?"

Tom grinned. "I had thought of calling it *Durastress*. How do you like that?"

Before anyone could comment, the telephone rang. Tom picked it up, spoke for a moment, then handed it to Sandy. "For you, Sis. Orton Throme."

"Just wanted to tell you how much I enjoyed the picnic the other day," the painter said, loudly enough for the others to hear.

"We enjoyed having you join us, Ort," said Sandy. She threw a glance at Bud, who reddened a bit and pretended to be engrossed in examining the test rods.

"I'd like you all to be *my* guests this evening," the painter went on. "The food will be simple, but I'm really a pretty good cook. Perhaps your brother could come along. I'd like to meet him."

After a hasty conference with Tom and the others, Sandy accepted, adding, "Why not drop over to the plant for lunch? Then we can all drive back to your cabin this evening."

"Great! I'll be there at noon!"

By the time lunch was over, Tom had taken a

thorough liking to the ex-Marine ace. Even Bud found it hard to resist Ort's dry, good-natured witticisms.

"If it won't bore you, maybe you'd like to watch me test my new atomic power plant," Tom suggested.

"Bore me? I'll get a real bang out of it," Ort said eagerly.

"Let's hope not!" Bud gulped, recalling the previous explosion.

A duplicate of the first power cell had been under construction ever since Tom and his companions had first arrived at the Citadel. It was now ready for testing. Meanwhile, following the successful strength tests of the Durastress that morning, a housing for the power capsule had been molded out of the new plastic.

Ort was immensely impressed when he saw the imposing steel-and-concrete pressure chamber in which the test would take place. Jutting from one wall were the huge gleaming pipes and columns of the hydraulic pressure gear.

Tom hooked up the assembled power capsule inside the chamber and clamped the view port shut. He twirled a valve, watching the pressure dial carefully, and finally switched on the atomic power plant.

"What's happening?" Ort murmured, as they all watched the window through dark goggles.

"The chamber pressure is the same as the pressure that's building up inside the atomic capsule," Tom replied.

A few minutes later, as the midget power plant reached its maximum working pressure, Tom added, "Now I'll start *reducing* the chamber pressure."

His eyes darted back and forth among several dials on the control panel as he slowly turned the hydraulic valve. The others watched tensely.

At last Tom gave a cry of triumph. "The pressure in the chamber is now normal atmospheric," he announced. "The capsule casing is sustaining the full pressure of the atomic reaction!"

The test continued smoothly, with the cell churning out its maximum electrical output.

Bud slapped the young inventor on the back. "Good work, pal! Your new Durastress plastic is a wonder!"

When the test was over, Tom cautiously disassembled the power capsule and inspected the casing. Even under X-ray examination, it showed no cracks or signs of failure.

Ort and the girls congratulated Tom, and Sandy added, "Now you can go ahead with your atomicar project!"

"I'll radio Enterprises and have the car flown out tonight," Tom replied.

Dinner that evening at Ort's adobe cottage-studio turned out to be a celebration for Tom. The red-haired painter's boast about his cooking proved to be more than justified. Even Bud was won over by Ort's delicious *tortillas*, fritters, and the crisp charcoal-broiled steaks.

"Good thing Chow isn't here," Bud said, grinning, "or he'd be turning green with envy!"

"I'll be surprised," said Tom, "if *you* don't turn green after the way you stoked up!"

The next day Ort and the others witnessed the atomicar's first test run under atomic power. Tom was jubilant over its smooth performance.

"I hate to cut this vacation short," he announced, "but I think we'd better fly back to Enterprises tonight. I must arrange the first public showing of the atomicar."

"Got room for another passenger?" Ort asked.

Tom was somewhat surprised, but willingly invited the painter to accompany them on the flight back East. The *Sky Queen* took off at dusk. As the huge plane streaked away from the last glow of a flaming sunset, Ort amused the girls by taking out a box of water colors and sketching a new body shell for the atomicar.

"Hey! Pretty snazzy!" said Bud, who had just come aft to join them in the comfortable lounge. "That's even better than—"

His words were cut short as the ship suddenly dived, throwing everyone off balance.

"Hang on, everyone!" Tom's voice barked over the intercom. "A strange jet's attacking us!"

CHAPTER VII

TOM TAKES A DARE

BEFORE Bud and the others could catch their breaths, the *Sky Queen* banked sharply. A split second later they were nearly deafened by an ear-splitting whine. A dark shape streaked past the windows of the lounge!

"Roarin' rockets!" Chow gasped. He staggered backward and nearly fell as the Flying Lab zoomed into a steep climb.

"Fasten your seat belts!" Bud snapped to him and the girls.

After making sure that the three were secure, Bud and Ort hurried out through the passageway to the flight compartment. Twice they had to cling desperately to the handrails to keep from being hurled off their feet.

When they finally reached the flight compartment, Bud asked furiously, "What in blazes is that nitwit trying to do?"

"Force us down," Tom said tersely.

The words were hardly out of his mouth when a flat, expressionless voice came over the radio speaker. *"This is your last warning. My jet is armed. If you do not turn around and land on the desert according to instructions, you will be shot down!"*

Off through the twilight, high at two o'clock, they could see the attacking jet circling for another pass.

Ort clenched his fists. "Man! What I'd give to have that joker lined up in my sights right now!"

The jet came screaming toward them. Tom held course as long as he dared, then suddenly poured power to the jet lifters. The *Sky Queen* shot upward like a rocket, just in time to avoid a burst of tracer fire. The enemy jet whined harmlessly past, below them.

"Whew!" Bud exclaimed.

Tom banked into a lightning climb, looped, and rolled out neatly to dodge the next pass. His brain was working at top speed as he scanned the sky ahead.

"Swift to jet!" he spoke into the microphone. "Hold your fire! We're ready to listen to instructions!"

"Ah! Now you are talking sense!" came the response. *"Turn your ship around and steer the same course I do! We shall fly wing to wing!"*

As he finished speaking, the enemy pilot began

to execute a leisurely turn. Instead of following suit, Tom gunned the forward jets to full power!

"I ordered you to turn!" the pilot screamed.

"I said we were ready to *listen* to instructions —not follow them!" Tom gibed back over the radio.

Another burst of tracer fire grazed the Flying Lab's tail as the craft streaked into a billowing cloud mass. Tom rammed the stick forward and the *Sky Queen* plummeted earthward. His eyes were glued to the altimeter needle.

"Put out all lights!" Tom ordered.

Bud flicked the master switch as they plunged through the dark overcast. At the last safe instant, Tom pulled out of the dive—then switched full power to the jet lifters. The *Sky Queen* shuddered and steadied into fixed position.

The sky was now hanging motionless in the darkness on jet lifters, at scarcely a thousand feet of altitude.

"Nice going!" Ort murmured to Tom. "Wish I'd had you for a wing man!"

"What now, skipper?" Bud asked.

"We'll lie doggo here for a while and hope our little playmate can't find us!"

Tom switched on the search radar. A blip of light on the scope showed the enemy jet passing overhead. It traced a zigzag course. Evidently the pilot was probing for them above the overcast.

"What if he has radar too?" Bud asked.

Tom grinned, his face barely visible in the glow from the instrument panel.

"We're a fixed point, remember, and fairly close to the ground, so he's not likely to read us on his scope. Besides," Tom added, "we're going to scram out of here the first chance we get!"

In a minute the enemy blip had disappeared from their screen as the jet passed far out of range. Tom, after reassuring the girls and Chow over the intercom, sent the *Sky Queen* streaking off on a roundabout course.

"I think we've lost them, Bud. Want to take over?"

"Okay."

Tom and Ort joined the others in the lounge. "Good grief!" said Phyl shakily, "Who do you suppose it was? Some lunatic?"

"Could be," Tom replied. "Anyhow, it's all over." He said nothing more about the mystery, since he did not want to alarm the girls further.

But Sandy shot her brother a bright-eyed glance. "If you ask me, he was after your new atomic power plant," she said shrewdly. "Seems to me a lot of people would like to get their hands on it!"

"That may be the answer," Tom admitted. His attention was caught by Ort's colored sketch. "Hey! What's this?"

"Ort sketched a new body shell for your atomi-car," Sandy explained. "Isn't it gorgeous?"

The drawing showed a sleek, scarlet racer that had the appearance of a wingless jet. Like Tom's present atomicar, it was of teardrop design. But the bubble enclosure flared into a single high fin, raking sharply aft.

Tom whistled admiringly. "The future on wheels! Are you an industrial designer too, Ort, as well as a painter?"

Ort grinned. "No, just doodling. Do you like it?"

"As an eye-catcher, it's got my buggy stopped cold," Tom said. "It would certainly look swell in our publicity photos."

"Okay, it's yours. My first automotive design masterpiece."

Tom chuckled as they shook hands. "You're in business, Ort! Get ready for a flock of orders when we unveil it to the press!"

Forty minutes later they landed at Enterprises. Ort graciously declined Sandy and Tom's invitation to stay at the Swift home overnight, saying he must catch the ten-o'clock flight out of Shopton to New York.

Early the next morning Tom hustled off to the plant and made a full report of the aerial attack to Harlan Ames.

The security chief was shocked.

"Why didn't you radio us immediately, Tom?"

"It wouldn't have done us much good—with that nut right on our tail," Tom pointed out with a rueful grin. "And after we shook him, I thought it was wiser to keep radio silence."

Ames nodded, frowning. "I guess you have a point there. Any clues to the plane's identity?"

"None at all—except that we think he was after my atomic capsule." Tom said. "Too bad the technical journals published those advance reports on it! No doubt an inquiry would be hopeless, Harlan, but how about checking with the Air Force and the CAA?"

The security chief promised to do so. He added that the police still had no leads on the gold-toothed stranger responsible for the airport bomb scare.

Tom went back to his laboratory and called Arvid Hanson, the hulking six-footer who crafted all the scale models of the Swift inventions.

"What's up, skipper?" Arv asked.

"I want a new body shell made for my atomicar." He showed him Ort Throme's sketch.

Arv's eyes widened in admiration. "Some dreamboat! This is going to be fun. How soon do you want it, Tom?"

"As fast as you and the sheet-metal shop can deliver the goods."

Arv considered a moment. "No blueprints, eh?

Well, give us forty-eight hours if you want a real slick paint job."

"Good enough," Tom said. "We'll mount it over the week end, and I'll set up a press conference and demonstration for Monday morning!"

As soon as Arv left the laboratory, Tom plunged into a flurry of activity. Press releases had to be prepared, invitations sent to all wire services and automotive editors, and a test track laid out, with a viewing stand for the spectators.

On Monday morning Swift Enterprises hummed with excitement. A throng of newsmen, press photographers, and television cameramen crowded the stand as Tom displayed the gleaming, new, scarlet atomicar and explained its operation.

"Sorry that I can't reveal the details of my atomic power plant," Tom told them. "However, it provides a smooth flow of power to a small electric motor at each wheel, without any need for a bulky or complicated transmission."

Tom proceeded to describe each feature of his amazing new vehicle. The name of the present model, he concluded, was the *Silent Streak*.

Next came a test run of the atomicar. This included a breath-taking demonstration of its flying and hedgehopping abilities. Tom wound up by skimming the roof of the Administration Building in full view of his audience, as the stand rocked with cheers and applause. Several of the newsmen, chosen by lot, were then allowed to try out the *Silent Streak* themselves.

"And now," Tom announced over his public-address microphone, "I'd like to show you a new repelatron anticrash device, which will be standard equipment on all atomicars.

"The *Silent Streak* and a heavy truck," he went on, "both operated by remote control, will be driven head-on toward each other at top speed."

In the atomicar was a robot steering device for the test. One young reporter, with a cigarette dangling from his lips, broke into a loud guffaw. "Looks as if you don't have much faith in your own invention, Swift!"

"What makes you think so?" Tom said.

"That robot steering gadget," the reporter taunted. "If your anticrash device is really foolproof, why not drive the car yourself?"

Tom eyed the reporter coolly. "Very well. I *will* drive it myself."

An apprehensive murmur arose from the spectators. As Tom gave orders for the robot steering device to be removed, Bud clutched his arm.

"You sure you know what you're doing, Tom?" he whispered. "There's bound to be *some* risk. That guy's just sore because he missed out when they drew lots!"

Tom murmured something to his copilot, who nodded and hurried off. Then the young scientist

donned a crash helmet, climbed into the *Silent
Streak,* and strapped himself into the driver's
seat with a safety belt. As he pressed a button to
close the canopy, Tom grinned and held up
crossed fingers to the spectators.

At a prearranged signal, the truck was started
by remote control half a mile up the track. At the
same moment, Tom gunned the atomicar.

The two vehicles sped toward each other along
the narrow track. The onlookers gasped in horri-
fied suspense as the car and truck accelerated to
blinding speed. A woman reporter shrieked and
fainted.

Within inches of a crash, the two vehicles
slammed to a halt and rebounded safely from each
other! There was a moment of awed silence.
Then the spectators burst into thunderous
cheers. "Tom!" Sandy cried out, when her
brother was able to break away from the applaud-
ing newsmen who had swarmed out on the track
to congratulate him. "Did you have to scare us
like that?" she demanded.

"I must admit you had us pretty worried, son,"
Tom Sr. confessed.

Mrs. Swift, Phyl, and the Newtons were still
looking somewhat pale and shaken.

Tom grinned apologetically. "I'm sorry, folks,
but there was really no danger."

"No danger!" Mr. Newton burst out. "Good
heavens, boy! You might have been killed if the

repelatron-force ray from your anticrash device hadn't stopped that truck!"

"Not really, Uncle Ned," Tom replied. "You see, I had Bud call the airfield control tower and

tell them to keep their big repelatron trained on the truck every second. If the anticrash device hadn't worked, the tower operator would have blasted the truck off the track!"

When the relieved laughter subsided, Mrs. Swift murmured, "In that case, Tom dear, we forgive you."

News interviews and floods of queries asking how soon the atomicar would be placed on the market kept Tom busy for the next few days.

On Thursday came a surprising telegram, inviting Mr. Swift and Tom to spend a week end at

a hunting lodge in the Adirondacks. It was signed "Asa Provard."

"That's the banker Ed told us about, Dad!" Tom said, after reading the wire.

"Hmm. I can't accept, since I'll be flying to Washington on that new rocket project," Mr. Swift said thoughtfully. "Why don't you and Bud go along and see what's on this fellow's mind?"

"Okay. What can we lose?"

Late Friday afternoon, Tom and Bud drove out on the Enterprises airfield. Shortly afterward, as prearranged, Provard's private plane arrived to pick them up. The sleek twin-engined craft landed and a red-haired figure stepped out to meet them.

Orton Throme! The boys were amazed.

CHAPTER VIII

A CHALLENGING
EXPEDITION

"FANCY meeting you here!" said Bud dryly as he shook hands with the artist-pilot.

Tom merely grinned. "Hi, Ort!"

"I suppose you're pretty surprised to see me." The ex-Marine ace looked a bit embarrassed. "Hop in, fellows. I'll tell you all about it after we take off."

The two boys climbed aboard and took seats inside the luxuriously fitted cabin. Ort put on a radio headset, revved the engines, and on signal from the tower, taxied along the runway for take-off.

When they were air-borne, he flashed the boys a grin. "I fly, off and on, for Asa Provard," Ort explained. "You see, Provard was mighty good to me when I first tried my hand at painting after I got out of service. He paid for two years of study in Paris and bought my paintings when no one else would."

In return, Ort continued, he often served as Provard's private pilot and carried out various assignments for him around the world.

"I'm beginning to think our meeting in New Mexico was no accident," Tom remarked.

Ort flushed. "You're right. I'd been planning a painting trip to the Southwest. Provard learned from the newspapers you'd be there, so he asked me to—well, sort of size you up. I even provoked Bud into a fight out on the mesa." The red-haired ace grinned apologetically. "Needless to say, my report was highly favorable."

"I'm curious," said Tom, "to know why Mr. Provard sent for me."

"Honestly, I don't know," Ort confessed. "All I can tell you is that he's the head of one of the biggest banks in New York. He has several other big-shot financiers waiting at his lodge to meet you."

Tom and Bud exchanged meaningful glances. Whatever Provard wanted, it must be highly important.

The flight took them over a green wilderness of rugged, forest-clad slopes and blue mountain lakes. Presently Ort murmured, "Here we are!" and set the plane down on an airstrip carved out of the mountainside.

Bud gave a whistle as they climbed down. "Some layout!"

Just below the airstrip stood a magnificent low rambling lodge built of rough-hewn logs and fieldstone. On one side lay a row of tennis courts, and on the other a huge swimming pool.

A bald-headed man, with twinkling blue eyes and gold-rimmed glasses, came strolling up the slope to greet them. He was wearing a polo shirt and khaki shorts.

"I'm Asa Provard," he announced, smiling and thrusting out his hand to Tom. "Delighted you were able to accept my invitation."

"Sorry my father wasn't able to make it," Tom said. "This is my friend, Bud Barclay."

When they reached the lodge, three other men, named Tompkyns, Ruthers, and Grane, were introduced to the boys. To Tom's surprise, there was no talk of business. Provard suggested a few sets of tennis. Later came a dip in the pool, a hearty leisurely dinner, and early bedtime.

After breakfast the next morning, Tom and Bud wandered into their host's gun room. The walls were lined with several racks of rifles and shotguns, with fishing and hunting trophies mounted overhead.

Bud idly picked out a foreign-made shotgun with damascened barrels and silver-ornamented stock. "What a beauty!" he murmured.

"Expensive enough, but not half so much gun as this good old American twelve-gauge semiautomatic," said Ort Throme, who had come up behind them.

Bud felt a surge of irritation. "You're quite an expert on a lot of things, aren't you, Ort?" he needled.

The painter grinned. "I'm not much of a hunter, but I do a bit of shooting."

Bud, who was a skillful marksman, decided that the time had come to show some of his own superiority. "How about shooting a few clay pigeons? We'll make it a match."

Ort agreed politely. Each chose a gun and they went outside. Tom volunteered to throw the targets from a hand trap.

Taking turns, Bud and Ort each hit five of the first ten targets. The next one Bud missed, while Ort scored another bull's-eye. Angry at himself, Bud missed two of the next four. Ort, however, continued to blast every clay pigeon thrown, with monotonous accuracy.

Bud began to perspire and turn red in the face. When the match was over, he had knocked down eighteen out of twenty-five targets. Ort had racked up a perfect score of twenty-five hits!

"You're probably off form today, Bud," he said good-naturedly. "I just had a lucky streak."

"Lucky my eye," grumbled Bud. "You're *good!*" Later, as he and Tom returned the pieces to the gun room, Bud mopped his brow. "Whew! I'm glad that little warfare wasn't for real!"

Tom chuckled and slapped his chum on the back. "I guess the moral of that little contest is never shoot against an ex-Marine!"

The rest of the morning was spent on a hike through the woods. Then, after a lunch of sizzling fried trout, Provard gathered his guests on a circle of lawn chairs outside the lodge.

"No doubt you're wondering what's behind this week-end invitation, Tom," the banker said.

"Frankly, sir, I am."

"I'll explain," Provard began. "My colleagues and I are underwriting a private foreign aid project of our own—with no assistance from Uncle Sam. We need the kind of technical help, however, that only you Swifts can provide."

The project, he went on, was an attempt to industrialize the new country of Kabulistan almost overnight. "Lift it by its bootstraps, so to speak," Provard added.

Kabulistan! Tom and Bud were excited by this announcement.

"Understand, we aren't starry-eyed idealists," put in Ruthers. "We're out to make a profit. But at the same time we believe we can help Kabulistan raise the living standards of its people— with no strings attached."

"Our aim," Provard said, "is to develop the country's resources as quickly as possible. This will mean building industrial plants, dams, roads, bridges, schools, and hospitals.

"We think the project is important to the whole free world," Provard added, "because if we don't succeed, Kabulistan may soon fall victim to some greedy foreign power. Certain neighboring countries are already being unduly friendly and offering technical help."

The banker said he and his group were only financiers—money men. They would need an engineering firm to mastermind and carry out such a big-scale technical program. All were agreed that Swift Enterprises was the scientific organization best fitted to tackle the job.

The talk went on throughout the afternoon and evening. Tom was thrilled by the scope of the project. On Sunday, before flying home, he gave Provard and group a tentative Yes on behalf of Swift Enterprises—subject to his father's approval.

When Mr. Swift, accompanied by Ned Newton, arrived home that evening, Tom said, "Dad, I think it's a wonderful chance to help the Kabulistanians. Also, it's a chance to *prove* how free scientific know-how can benefit all humanity."

"What's your opinion, Ned?" Mr. Swift asked.

Mr. Newton frowned thoughtfully. "Our setup may be strained for time and men if that new rocket program comes through," he said. "But I agree with Tom. This project is something we can't afford to pass up."

Mr. Swift's blue eyes brightened. "Glad you think so, Ned, because I agree wholeheartedly," he said. Turning back to Tom, he added more seriously, "This will be a terrific undertaking, son, and you'll have to bear the brunt of it. But I'm confident you'll do an A-1 job."

"Thanks, Dad." Tom's voice was quiet, but his heart was pounding.

"It's settled, then," his father concluded. "Ned, suppose you get in touch with Provard and see about drawing up a contract."

The next two days were spent in feverish activity. As a first step, Tom had decided to make a quick survey trip to Kabulistan to familiarize himself with the country. Supplies were ordered and loaded aboard the *Sky Queen*. Besides Bud and Chow Winkler, Tom chose Arv Hanson, Hank Sterling, the blond, square-jawed chief patternmaking engineer of Enterprises, and a lanky Swift test pilot named Slim Davis to accompany him on the flight.

Taking off Wednesday morning, the Flying Lab streaked over the Atlantic Ocean to Europe and the Middle East into Iran, then across the central plateau and Eastern Persian Highlands to the rugged little land of Kabulistan.

Its capital city of Shirabad lay spread out along

the sloping floor of a mountain valley. Sunlight twinkled from its whitewashed buildings and tile-domed mosques.

"Sure don't look like much of an airfield," Chow grumbled as Tom prepared to land.

Bud agreed. "Looks as though they just finished hacking it out with a bulldozer."

In spite of the field's size and badly paved runways, a surprising number of planes were clustered on it. At a signal from the tower, the *Sky Queen* touched down on its jet lifters.

"What's this—a welcoming committee?" Hank Sterling murmured to Tom as they climbed out.

A number of soldiers, in ill-fitting khaki uniforms and armed with rifles, came rushing out of the airport building toward them. Before Tom and his friends knew what was happening, the soldiers were grabbing them roughly.

"Oh, no, you don't, buckaroo!" Chow bellowed, lashing out at a soldier who laid hands on him.

A rifle butt whacked the chef on his head, and Chow exploded. In a moment a wild melee had broken out!

CHAPTER IX

MYSTERIOUS HOSTILITY

ENRAGED by the blow dealt to Chow, Tom and his friends fought back vigorously, punching and elbowing right and left. The soldiers, meanwhile, milled about in a tight tangle, swinging their rifles with hoarse, angry shouts.

Arv's beefy fists sent one man sprawling, while Hank doubled up a wild-eyed sergeant with a right to the solar plexus. Slim almost went down with his forehead bloodied by a slashing rifle butt. Bud, angrier than ever, sailed into Slim's assailant like a fiery-eyed gamecock.

Tom realized that the whole project might be ruined before they had scarcely glimpsed Kabulistan. "Everybody hold it! Stop!" he shouted frantically.

After repeated pleas and gestures, Tom finally managed to calm the combatants. "No sense starting a war the minute we land," he pointed out to his companions. "Besides, we can't take on their whole army. Let's go along peaceably and find out what this is all about."

Reluctantly the others followed his example and allowed themselves to be taken in charge. The soldiers promptly herded the visitors aboard a truck and drove them to a nearby Army barracks.

A colonel with a black mustache glanced up and glowered fiercely as they were marched into his office. "Ah, yes! The prisoners!" he said in English with a heavy accent.

"What's the meaning of this outrage?" Tom demanded, stepping up boldly. "We land here on a technical mission to help your country, and your soldiers attack us without cause!"

The colonel stared at Tom in surprise. Then he stroked his mustache and sneered.

"Technical mission, eh? That, of course, is your story. Unfortunately for you, we have already been—how do you say?—*tipped off* that you are dangerous enemy spies."

This time, it was Tom's turn to gape in surprise. Recovering, he burst out laughing.

"I guess your soldiers can prove that we *are* rather dangerous," Tom said, "even though we're completely unarmed—"

"Unarmed? Is this true?" the colonel asked the sergeant in charge.

The officer nodded sheepishly.

"As for our being spies," Tom went on, "we have visaed passports and papers signed by your own ambassador in Washington, *inviting* us to come here at the request of your ruler."

The colonel frowned and stroked his jaw as Tom took out a sheaf of credentials, many stamped with elaborate gold seals. Reading them over, one by one, the colonel flushed and began to perspire heavily. Suddenly he sprang up.

"Salmut-e-Salaam!" he exclaimed, bowing and snapping his heels. "It is clear there has been some mistake in our information, and I apologize most deeply. Colonel Kazar, at your service!"

Chow and the others grinned. Tom smiled and shook hands with the officer.

"By the way, sir, do you mind telling us who provided the false information about us?"

The colonel stroked his mustache and looked uncomfortable. "Um—ah—it was received by telephone," he mumbled. "Most unfortunate. I should prefer to say no more about it. But rest assured that suitable action will be taken against those responsible."

Tom guessed that the call had been anonymous, and although very curious as to the identity of the culprit, felt that it would be wiser to let the matter drop.

"In any case, Colonel, we're due at the palace for a royal audience," he went on. "Perhaps one of your men could show us the way."

The colonel leaped into action. He barked out orders and the sergeant bolted off on a run. Moments later a large, glistening, but somewhat antiquated limousine was driven up to the front door of the barracks.

Colonel Kazar escorted the five Americans out, with profuse apologies and compliments. The sergeant helped them climb aboard. Tom's companions chuckled as the car pulled away.

"Brand my flapjacks!" Chow declared. "I'll bet we left *that* hombre stewin'!"

The palace was a large white building topped by graceful minarets and a gleaming, jewellike dome. After an hour's wait, Tom's group was ushered into an office richly furnished with satin draperies, upholstered chairs, and an Oriental rug.

Habib Shah, the Western-educated ruler of Kabulistan, rose from his desk to greet them.

"I am most grateful," he said to Tom, "that you have come to help my people with your scientific prowess. Even in Kabulistan we have heard of the exploits of the two famous Tom Swifts."

Tom flushed slightly. "Thank you, Your Majesty."

The Shah shook hands with each man in the group, then turned back to Tom. "You are free to survey and inspect the entire country at will. Come to me at any time you need assistance."

"We'll do our best to justify your confidence, sir," Tom replied.

On their way out of the palace, Tom's group went through an anteroom crowded with people. Tom noticed a gaunt, black-bearded man pacing back and forth. He was wearing a ruby tie clasp!

"That's Nurhan Flambo!" Tom whispered to Bud.

At that moment Flambo caught sight of Tom. His hawklike eyes flashed angrily as he strode forward.

"So!" he hissed. "It is clear now why you refused my offer! I have heard about the cunning project by which you seek to gain a business advantage here in the Middle East!"

Bud was about to retort when Tom stopped him. "If you've heard about our project, Mr. Flambo," Tom said calmly, "then you know we were invited here by the Shah. Come on, fellows!"

Outside the palace, Bud said hotly, "Ten to one he was the sneak who gave the colonel that phony tip about our being spies!" Hank and the others were inclined to agree, but Tom refused to jump to conclusions.

Tom hailed a rickety taxi and the group returned to the airport long enough for Chow to serve them a dinner of steak and French fried potatoes aboard the *Sky Queen*. Then Tom, Bud, and Arv Hanson sauntered out to explore the town, leaving Hank, Slim, and the Texan to guard the plane.

Shirabad was a strange jumble of the old and new. Ancient mosques and houses of sun-baked mud or brick stood within sight of modern three-story buildings. Many of the streets were unpaved, yet flashy-looking automobiles sped past donkey carts and bearded camel drivers.

"Quite a contrast!" Arv remarked.

Veiled women and fierce-faced men in turbans and baggy trousers rubbed shoulders with hurrying Europeans in well-cut business suits.

"Provard and his partners must have beat out a lot of competition to land this deal with the Shah," Bud remarked.

Tom said thoughtfully, "I guess that's why Flambo was so sore."

The bazaar, which was the local market place, was a dirt-floored arcade, covered over by an arching brick roof. Tom and his two companions strolled inside. The narrow lane was lined with booths and stalls where craftsmen and merchants displayed their wares.

"Hey! A bookstall!" Bud said. The boys, intrigued, stopped to examine the volumes, some of which were old, and many printed in different languages.

Tom became excited as he noticed one old book entitled *Jewels of the East*. He flipped through its pages as the proprietor stood by eagerly. The volume was written in English and had been printed in 1810.

"Look!" Tom exclaimed. "Here's a chapter on famous ruby mines!" Turning to the proprietor, he asked the price.

The shop owner started to name a sum, but suddenly paled and stopped short with a gasp. "N-no! The book is not for sale!" he mumbled.

Tom, suspicious that the man had suddenly been intimidated, whirled just in time to see a tall, sinister-looking, turbaned native not far away. He was scowling and fingering a knife at his belt. As he caught Tom's glance, the stranger vanished hastily among the crowd of shoppers.

"We want to buy this book! How much?" Bud persisted. But the proprietor no longer seemed to understand English. He shook his head, snatched the book away, and thrust it out of sight.

The boys, their interest thoroughly aroused, continued to argue. But the shop owner remained adamant. Finally Tom and Bud gave up, and left.

Thinking over the incident in his bunk aboard the *Sky Queen* that night, Tom felt sure the book might contain a clue to the Amir's Mine. The next morning he and Bud decided to return to the bazaar, and headed for the bookseller's stall. To the boys' astonishment, it was shuttered and empty! They tried to question the merchants nearby, but received no enlightening answers.

Suddenly a voice behind the boys asked, "Trying to buy something?"

Tom turned in surprise. A huge, ruddy-cheeked man with a blond handlebar mustache grinned and stuck out his hand. "Mr. Wayne! I didn't expect to meet you here," Tom said, and introduced Bud to Simon Wayne.

The man chuckled. "I get around. Came here to land some business for Europa Fabrik! What about yourself?"

Tom replied guardedly and changed the subject by mentioning the incident with the bookseller.

"Hmm." Wayne frowned and twirled his mustache. "That fellow who scared the proprietor may have been a member of the Assassins cult."

This, he went on, was a group of religious fanatics who specialized in murder. The leader of the sect, known as "The Old Man of the Mountains," had once had his stronghold in the Kabulistan highlands.

"Did the book have anything to do with the mountainous interior of the country?" Wayne asked.

Tom hesitated. "Yes, in a way."

"That probably explains it," Wayne said. "I've heard rumors the cult is active again, and trying to keep outsiders from learning anything about the territory where they hide."

Bud shot an uneasy glance at Tom. Later, after they had parted from Wayne, Bud remarked with a gulp, "Let's hope we don't get our throats cut, poking around these hills!"

As soon as they returned to the airport, Tom laid out a plan of action. Hank would stay in Shirabad that day to see about recruiting local workmen for the project. Meanwhile, Tom and the others would take off in the *Sky Queen* for a survey flight over the mountain-girded country.

Soon they were winging across the rugged interior. The steppes and plateaus were almost barren, but there were pasture lands and farm villages on the upward slopes, watered by melting snows from the peaks.

Retracing their route, Tom picked out a site for his base camp near a winding river. He set the *Queen* down vertically on its jet lifters and a small amount of equipment was unloaded. Tom, Bud, and Chow were to set up camp here long enough to investigate the area, while Arv and Slim flew back to Shirabad to meet Hank.

As dusk fell, the three Americans ate a supper of canned beef and potatoes cooked over a blazing campfire.

"Oh—oh! We ain't alone, boss," Chow said suddenly. His keen eyes had detected a movement on the skyline.

Tom conned the cliffs through binoculars and made out at least two figures—evidently lookouts watching the camp. The darkness deepened. Suddenly a flare shot up from the cliffs.

Was it a signal? Were the campers about to be attacked?

CHAPTER X

MAGNETIC HOMING
PIGEON

TENSELY Bud eyed the cliffs from which the flare had appeared.

"What if they jump us?" he asked.

Tom tried to sound more confident than he felt. "No reason why they should. We haven't harmed anyone, and so far as I know, the people inhabiting these mountains aren't hostile to strangers."

"I sure wouldn't call it friendly—the way them sidewinders is spyin' on us," Chow grumbled. He scratched his stubby chin thoughtfully, then added, "On the other hand, Injuns out West used to spy on wagon trains without attackin'."

The darkness and silence grew nerve-racking. The only sounds were the chirping of insects and an occasional distant screech of a hunting hawk.

Tom warmed up the battery-powered radio set and tried to contact the *Sky Queen*. But his calls brought no response.

98

"Arv and Slim might be in town looking for Hank," Tom muttered as he gave up. "Or else they've gone to bed."

An hour went by, then another, with still no signs of an attack.

"Mebbe them owlhoots are waitin' for us to hit the hay," Chow surmised.

"Just what I'm thinking," said Bud. "Better keep awake."

The night was turning more and more chilly. The three friends sat huddled in sleeping bags as they watched and waited. A rising moon etched the cliffs sharply against the night sky, but no further signal flares appeared.

Tom poked up the fire and tossed on some more wood. Presently the trio caught themselves dozing off. By this time their confidence had returned somewhat, so Tom suggested that they take turns standing watch. "I'll start. You two sleep."

"Okay by me," Bud said wearily. Chow agreed.

The night passed slowly, with no further incident. In the fresh pearly light of dawn, they washed at the riverside, then ate breakfast. Cheerfulness returned with the rising sun, and all three felt somewhat foolish about their fears of the night before. The lookouts seemed to have vanished from the cliffs—at least none could be detected through binoculars.

"It's a cinch someone's interested in our movements, though," Tom reflected soberly.

Later that morning Arv, Hank, and Slim arrived from Shirabad in the *Sky Queen*.

"Our radio conked out last night," Arv explained, after hearing about Tom's vain attempt to contact them. "Turned out to be a blown condenser, but we had so much trouble tracing it down we let the repair job go until this morning. Sorry, skip."

"No harm done," Tom said with a chuckle, "but our nerves got a slight workout."

Hank reported that he had engaged an interpreter with whose aid he had rounded up a number of workmen, ready to start as soon as needed.

"Good work, Hank," Tom said. "Let's hope they'll catch on to what we want done."

After mapping the camp site carefully and making another brief survey flight, Tom set the *Sky Queen* on course back to Shopton. Stars studded the night sky as they winged homeward across the Atlantic.

"Let's see. That there's the Big Dipper, ain't it?" said Chow, peering off to starboard. "And that star right above it is the North Star."

"Go to the head of the class, pardner," said Tom, smiling.

"I guess sailors an' avvy-ators don't have to steer by the North Star any more—like folks used to in the ole days—do they, Tom?"

"That's right." Tom grinned. "Still nice to

have it up there, though. But we do have pretty reliable compasses these days."

Chow scratched his bald dome. "Never can keep straight how them thingamabobs work."

Tom explained that a magnetic compass needle kept pointing toward the poles through the lines of force exerted by the earth. In turn, the earth acts as a natural magnet. A gyrocompass, on the other hand, is like a spinning top which always stays lined up in one direction.

"Trouble is, a critter don't often head straight for the North or South Pole," Chow reflected. "Too bad there ain't no simple way for a ship or airyplane to always point straight home—or wherever 'tis it's aimin' for."

Tom was thoughtful for a few moments. "You know, you've got something there, Chow," he said. "A sure-fire homing device would come in mighty handy to navigators."

At Enterprises the next day Tom reported to his father and Uncle Ned the results of his Kabulistan trip. "I think my new atomic power plant can be a big help in developing the country," the young inventor said. "We can place it easily, anywhere, to provide electricity for factories and villages."

"Very good," Mr. Swift replied, and Uncle Ned added, "The capsule alone will save the time and expense of building dams or steam generating plants."

"I've already given orders for a production run of one hundred capsules out at the Citadel," Mr. Swift added.

"Swell, Dad. And by the way, Uncle Ned— speaking of production runs, how about setting up an assembly line for a fleet of atomicars and trucks at the Swift Construction Company?"

Tom explained that these should prove invaluable to project crews in traveling around the rugged terrain and also transporting supplies. Ned Newton promised to attend to the matter at once.

"Exactly what are Kabulistan's natural resources, son?" Mr. Swift asked.

Tom read off a brief report which the Shah's economic minister had drawn up at Provard's request. "Doesn't add up to very much in trade dollars," Tom ended, "unless you count that lost ruby mine. The trouble is, Dad, that nobody really knows the country's potential resources, but there must be valuable mineral deposits."

"Any ideas on the quickest way to find them?" the elder scientist inquired.

Tom nodded. "The fastest way would be by aerial prospecting."

To accomplish this, Tom went on, he proposed to build a fleet of small atomic-powered drone planes. These would carry Tom's detecting Damonscope to spot radioactive ore, and his father's mineral detectors. By sending the drones out in a search pattern across the whole country, it would be possible to locate any deposits quickly.

"But if you're using unmanned drone planes, how do you expect to map the deposits?" Ned Newton asked with a puzzled frown.

Tom grinned. "Chow gave me the idea last night—a magnetic homing device."

Tom sketched his plan on paper. Each plane would carry a magnetic sensing unit—trailed through the air at the end of a cable. This would "sense" the patterns of terrestrial magnetism which the plane passed over.

These patterns would be recorded on a magnetic memory drum, connected to a master steering unit inside the plane. When the drum was "played back" through the master unit, the plane would automatically retrace its course to home base.

"Each plane will beep a radio signal whenever it detects a mineral deposit," Tom said. "This will start the playback. And when the plane returns to base, we simply check its flight course as recorded on tape to get the location of the deposit."

Both Mr. Swift and Uncle Ned were enthusiastic.

"A mechanical homing pigeon," Tom's father added.

Tom drove back to his laboratory and set to work at once designing his newest invention. In two days, a pilot model of his drone plane was ready. It was a sleek and simple six-foot craft. Its propeller was driven by electricity generated from a midget model of Tom's atomic power plant.

Twenty-four hours later his magnetic homing device was ready for a test. The next day Tom and Bud took off from Enterprises in a small helicopter and landed on a hillside about a hundred miles northwest of Shopton.

"Okay! Let 'er rip!" Tom radioed back to Hank Sterling at the plant, after giving their precise position.

Hank fed the position into a pocket-sized flight-course computer which was hooked up to the master steering unit. Then he watched the little drone plane take off from the airfield.

In twenty minutes it landed gracefully on the hillside where Tom and Bud were waiting. Tom opened the fuselage and switched the magnetic memory drum into playback.

"So far, so good," Tom murmured. "Now to see if our little homing pigeon really knows its way home."

The boys stood back and watched hopefully as the drone zoomed aloft. Seconds later, they were open-mouthed in dismay. Instead of heading toward Shopton, the mechanical pigeon went out of sight beyond the hills!

CHAPTER XI

CALLING ALL HAMS!

"WHAT happened to the homing pigeon?" Bud gasped.

"You've got me, pal!" Tom admitted. "We can figure that out later. The important thing now is to find out where it lands! Come on!"

Tom raced for the helicopter, with Bud at his heels. They hopped aboard and Tom gunned the rotor. As they soared above the hillside, the boys could see the little drone plane already a distant speck in the sky.

"Give her more juice, skipper, or we'll lose it!" Bud pleaded.

"We're making all the speed I can nurse out of this eggbeater!" Tom groaned. "Wish I'd taken a helijet instead of this crate!"

By the time their craft had crossed the highest ridge in the range of hills, the drone plane had completely disappeared from view. Tom flicked on the radio and reached for his microphone. "Tom calling Enterprises! Come in, please!" As a voice crackled in response, Tom asked, "Are you tracking the drone on radar?"

"Trying to, Tom," replied Hank. "We can barely keep locked on. Something's gone haywire—that homing pigeon's flying a crazy, zigzag course!"

Hank's reports continued, moment by moment. Then came the final word. "Out of range, skipper. We've lost it."

Tom was stunned. As the boys headed back to the experimental station, Bud broke the gloomy silence. "What do you think went wrong—the homing device, or the control system?"

Tom shrugged. "There are a dozen possibilities." An angry light blazed in his steel-blue eyes. "But hang it, Bud, the plane was completely checked out this morning. I just can't see how it could have flown such a goofy course . . . unless . . ."

Bud shot him a startled glance. "Unless what?"

"Well, unless someone jammed the master steering unit by radio impulses."

"Oh—oh!" Bud gave a low whistle. "You mean sabotage?"

"Worse than that," Tom said. "If someone could jam it, why not go a step further and radio new instructions to the steering circuits? That would explain the zigzag course—an attempt to foul us up in tracking it while it's being guided to some secret landing spot!"

Hank Sterling met the boys as their helicopter landed on the Enterprises airfield.

"I have half a dozen jet crews lined up and standing by for an aerial search, Tom," the blond engineer reported. "Dilling's checking with the CAA and the Civil Air Patrol."

George Dilling, an ace radio expert, was the Enterprises communications chief.

"Good work, Hank," Tom said. "Did you plot the drone's course?"

"As far as we tracked it."

Tom hurried to Hangar C with Hank and Bud. Tom studied the chart on which Hank had penciled in the drone plane's movements.

"What a mess! This will be like looking for a needle in a haystack!" Tom frowned in deep concentration, figuring his next move. "No telling how far the bird will fly, either, before she comes down! Well, we'll just have to play it by ear."

The young inventor issued quick instructions to the flight crews. Hank Sterling and Slim Davis would be piloting two of the search jets. Tom took off with Bud in a helijet.

This sleek craft, one of Tom's earlier inventions, was known as a Whirling Duck. It had pulse-jet rotors for vertical take-off or hovering, but could also operate as a conventional jet plane with its rotors folded into the fuselage.

The aerial search ranged over several states. Tom kept in constant touch by radio with the other pilots, as each combed a separate area. By late afternoon all had drawn a total blank.

"Guess it's hopeless, fellows," Tom radioed at last to his search pilots. "Go on back to base."

"*Roger!*". . ."*Tough luck, skipper!*" the pilots acknowledged, one by one.

Grim-faced and weary, Tom and Bud returned to Enterprises. The young inventor called an immediate conference at the Security Building with Ames, Hank Sterling, and George Dilling. Bud was also on hand.

"Looks as though we're up against a blank wall —for a while, anyhow," said Hank gloomily. "If your homing device crashed in a swamp or some wooded area, it may not be spotted for days."

"And if the bird's been hijacked, it's probably under cover by this time," put in Bud with a scowl.

Harlan Ames glanced keenly at the young inventor, who was pacing back and forth. "What's your own guess, Tom?"

"I'm willing to bet the whole thing was no accident." Tom was tight-lipped. "Ten to one Bud hit it right on the nose."

Ames frowned and nodded. "Hijacked by the same enemy who buzzed the *Sky Queen,* no doubt."

"Right. And for the same reason," Tom said.

"To get his hands on my atomic power plant. Harlan, any competitor who copies that before ours is on the market can cut himself in on a fortune!"

Tom resumed his restless pacing. "If only there were some way to contact—"

"Wait a second, skipper!" George Dilling spoke up suddenly. "Isn't the master unit on that drone designed for radio monitoring?"

"Sure." Tom paused. "I designed it that way for mineral survey flights later on in Kabulistan. Unfortunately that's what made it vulnerable to enemy interception."

Dilling stabbed the air with his finger. "Okay, and that also means it should respond to a radio request pulse from *us* here at Enterprises!"

"Hey! You're right!" Tom exclaimed, his face lighting up. "And if we can get a fix by triangulation on the response pulse, we can locate the plane!"

"We'll get it all right," Dilling declared. "I know half the radio hams east of the Mississippi —not to mention out West! They'll all be glad to help us."

Tom gave the radio chief an excited bear hug. "George, old boy, you're a genius! As the designer, I rate a kick for not thinking of that myself!"

The entire group hurried to the Enterprises communications center. Here, Dilling began beaming out a general call for assistance to all radio amateurs. Almost immediately, the hams began checking in by call letters. By the time Chow wheeled in a supper of hot roast beef sandwiches, more than a hundred responses had been received. Many promised to alert their friends and amateur club groups.

Dilling explained that a high-flying plane over Enterprises would beam out a "request" pulse once per minute, beginning at seven o'clock and continuing until a fix had been obtained. Hank was dispatched to perform this job in a helijet.

Tom glanced nervously at his watch as the hands ticked closer to seven.

"Relax, skipper." Bud chuckled and slapped his friend on the back. "How can we miss?"

"We can't, unless our enemy has tinkered with the homing device."

Bud's face grew taut. "Cut it out. Now you've got *my* pulse missing!"

Within minutes after seven o'clock, more than a dozen radio bearings had been received. Dilling, too, had picked up the response pulse, faint but clear.

"Good enough! We have it practically pinpointed!" Tom exclaimed, as he ruled the last bearing line on the chart.

All were surprised by the position of the fix— a point almost on the seacoast, about one hundred and seventy miles southeast of Shopton.

A shattering blast threw the helijet about like a toy!

Tom announced he would take off at once for the spot, in spite of Harlan Ames's worried words of caution.

"The longer we wait, the more time our enemy will have to figure out the construction of my atomic power plant," Tom pointed out. "Besides, we have only about an hour of daylight left."

Tom decided that if he ran into trouble while scouting, he would radio for reinforcements at once. Moments later, he and Bud took off in a helijet. Both boys were tense and excited as they streaked southeastward through the sky.

"That must be it," Tom muttered presently.

Just ahead, between a coastal highway and a sandy stretch of open beach, lay a large barnlike building. Tom hovered in low.

"Think we should land?" Bud asked.

A split second later the barn exploded in a shattering blast that threw the helijet about like a toy!

CHAPTER XII

RADIOACTIVE!

THE terrific concussion stunned both boys, like a blow from a club. Bud blacked out as the helijet spun through the air. Tom, clinging to the controls, struggled to maintain a glimmer of consciousness.

Somehow, Tom brought the craft under partial control and managed to land it safely on the beach. But the strain proved too much for his dazed senses. The helijet's wheels had barely touched the sand when he felt consciousness slipping away.

Bud groaned faintly and started to revive. As his eyes flickered open, he saw his chum slumped over the controls.

"Tom! Are you all right?"

Frantically Bud gave his friend what first aid he could. Gradually Tom revived.

"Good night! What hit us?" Tom murmured.

He sat upright. "Oh—oh! I remember now! That blast!"

Both boys turned and stared in horror at a reddish glow on their right. A quarter of a mile up the beach, the barnlike building was now a tumbled mass of ruins. Vivid flames and billowing smoke shot from one end of the wreckage.

Bud gasped. Then his eyes narrowed. "Do you suppose the place was booby-trapped, skipper? We might have broken a magnetic field and triggered off the blast as we came down!"

Tom shuddered. "It's possible, all right." Grabbing the microphone, he warmed up the radio and contacted Enterprises. After making a quick report on what had happened, Tom added:

"Call the nearest town and have them rush fire-fighting equipment! And send a cargo jet here pronto with gear to probe the wreckage! Better include some antiradiation suits—the ruins may be radioactive if the drone was inside when the blast went off!"

"Roger!"

The boys climbed out of the Whirling Duck and approached the scene as closely as they dared.

Suddenly Bud grabbed Tom's arm and pointed toward the ground. "Take a look!"

In spite of the gathering dusk, the fresh tracks of heavy-duty truck tires could be seen in the light of the blaze. The truck had passed over a rutted dirt lane connecting the building to the main highway. What caught the boys' eyes was a piece of galvanized iron roofing which had been ripped off the building by the blast. The tires had passed *over* it!

"You're right, Bud," Tom exclaimed. "Someone must have pulled away from here *after* the blast, while we were unconscious!" Tom added with a thoughtful frown, "Which means the blast must have been accidental—not a booby trap."

Within moments, screaming sirens heralded the arrival of fire trucks. An ambulance sped to the scene close behind them. Pumps were set up on the beach and fire hoses played streams of sea water over the blazing ruins.

Just as the last flames were quenched, a Swift cargo jet streaked into view. It lowered onto the sand by its jet lifters, and half a dozen Enterprises men climbed out. Among them were Hank Sterling, Harlan Ames, and Arv Hanson.

"Open the hatch and get out that portable crane," Hank ordered his assistants.

Tom and the others hastily donned hooded antiradiation coveralls. As they approached the still-smoking wreckage, the red lights on their suit meters flashed a warning.

"The place is radioactive, all right," Bud muttered.

The firemen—and spectators who had stopped along the highway—were warned back. Then Hank supervised his crane crew, all in antiradiation suits, in the job of clearing away the debris to look for victims.

Tom and Bud, inspecting the undamaged part of the building, found two unconscious men, both wearing once white laboratory coats. The boys helped carry them to the ambulance.

Both victims were badly injured. One of the two was a stocky, balding individual with a sandy fringe of hair. The other was tall and dark, with a swarthy complexion.

As the latter was lifted into the ambulance, he moaned and his jaw sagged. Tom gasped as he saw that the man had several gold teeth. Was he the one who had caused the airport bomb scare?

"Will they live?" Bud asked the young intern who had examined the victims.

The medic shrugged. "Hard to say. They're both in bad shape. They certainly won't be able to answer any questions for a while."

The crane crew continued working, with the scene lit up by floodlights. Probing through the part of the building where the blast had centered, Tom found numerous parts and twisted structural members of his drone plane. He also discovered the blackened shell of the atomic capsule's Durastress casing.

But the most surprising find came half an hour later—the tattered remnants of a quaint-looking volume entitled *Travels in Remotest Araby!*

"Cousin Ed's book!" Tom exclaimed excitedly,

as he picked it out of the debris and shook off the soot and ashes. "I must show this to him!"

Ed Longstreet was due in Shopton the next day. When he arrived, Tom, who was in Harlan Ames's office, requested that Ed be sent there. He showed his cousin the book, which had proved to be not dangerously contaminated. Ed leafed through it, then his face darkened.

"A number of pages have been torn out!" he said. "The vital ones! Those that told about the Amir's Mine!"

Ames showed him a photograph. "Have you ever seen this man before?" the security chief asked. It was a picture, taken at the hospital, of the Arabian-featured victim.

Ed whistled and nodded. "The man who sat next to me on the plane to Shopton—Mr. Gold-tooth! By the way, what caused the blast?"

"Probably the atomic capsule blew up when they removed it from the drone and tried to dis-assemble it," Tom replied. "The casing was still intact."

"At least you have one more proof that your Durastress is the real McCoy," Ames put in.

Just then the telephone rang. Ames answered, spoke for a few minutes, then hung up. "That was the hospital," he reported. "Those two men are still unconscious and it's doubtful either will survive. The doctor says they absorbed pretty massive doses of radiation."

One thing seemed certain. The same enemy had engineered the theft of both the old book and the drone plane. Hence, Tom reasoned, whoever was trying to ferret out the secret of his atomic power plant was also involved in the ruby mine mystery.

"And I have a hunch we'll find the answer to both riddles in Kabulistan!" Tom declared.

As the meeting broke up, the young inventor felt more eager than ever to press ahead with Provard's Middle Eastern project. Refusing to be discouraged by the loss of his homing drone, Tom set to work constructing a new model of both the plane and the homing device. This time, Tom included a safe but effective "destroy" mechanism which would sabotage instantly all secret parts if anyone tampered with the plane.

Forty-eight hours later the homing pigeon tested out successfully—the magnetic homing device guiding it straight back to the plant. Tom was jubilant over the success of his latest invention.

When he arrived back at his laboratory, he was informed that Asa Provard was calling on the phone. "Something terrible has happened!" the banker cried. "We must give up the Kabulistan project!"

CHAPTER XIII

THE FURTIVE JEWELER

"YOU mean call the whole thing off?" Tom could hardly believe his ears.

"I'm afraid we have no choice," Provard replied. His voice sounded hoarse and strained.

"But why, sir?"

"I—I think it wiser not to discuss the matter over the phone," the banker told Tom. "Will you be at your experimental station for the rest of the morning?"

"Yes."

"Very well. I'll take off for your place by plane as soon as possible."

Tom hung up in a daze. He had thrown himself so wholeheartedly into the project that he was shocked by Provard's announcement. A dazzling chance to show how the wonders of science could benefit a whole country, almost overnight—shattered by a single brief telephone call.

When Bud strolled into the laboratory a few

minutes later, he found the young inventor staring dejectedly out the window. "Hey! What cooks?" Bud inquired. "Whatever it is, it can't be *that* bad—not after your homing device just checked out perfectly!"

"Oh, no?" Tom retorted. "Wait'll you hear the latest news from Provard." He related the banker's startling message.

Bud listened with growing dismay. "But Provard can't just cancel the whole deal after all the spadework you've put into it! What does your dad think?"

"He went to Washington. But I sure wish he were here."

The banker's twin-engined private plane arrived from New York City forty minutes later. Mr. Provard was driven to the Swifts' office in the Administration Building. Tom, Bud, and Harlan Ames were on hand to meet him.

"I realize this decision comes as a blow," Provard began, when all were seated. "But after you hear what has happened, I think you'll agree there's nothing else we can do. You recall meeting Schuyler Grane, one of my three partners in the project, when you were up at the lodge?"

"Yes," said Tom and Bud.

"Well, he flew to Kabulistan two days ago to confer on financial details of the project," Provard went on. "Last night he was kidnaped from his hotel."

"What!" Tom and his friends were shocked.

Ames bent forward sharply. "Any idea who's responsible?"

"None at all," Provard replied. "I received the news by cable from the Kabulistan government this morning. Then, a short time later, I received an anonymous phone message."

The caller had warned that unless the Kabulistan technical aid project were completely abandoned, Provard's partner would never be seen alive again. There also would be further deadly reprisals.

Provard paused, took off his gold-rimmed glasses, and polished them nervously. His normally twinkling blue eyes were clouded with worry. "You understand I simply cannot go on. Schuyler Grane is not only my partner in this project—he's an old, dear friend. His wife and family are already crushed by this terrible news."

Tom's face was somber. "I appreciate your position, sir. And I agree that Mr. Grane's life mustn't be jeopardized."

In spite of his steady voice, Tom was inwardly blazing with anger.

"You've notified the police, I suppose?" he asked. "I mean—in connection with the anonymous phone call."

Provard nodded. "And also the FBI. But naturally there's little they can do, with the victim in a foreign country thousands of miles away."

"Do you suppose it's the same enemy who's been after your midget atomic power plant, Tom?" Bud spoke up.

The young inventor frowned and drummed his fingers on the desk. "Could be. What do you think, Harlan?"

"Offhand, I'd say Yes," the security chief replied. "It's clear we're up against a deadly and technically well-equipped foe who'll stop at nothing. I'd guess they're either foreign subversives, or powerful business competitors."

"Flambo!" Bud exploded, slamming his fist down on the desk.

"Don't forget," Tom said, "that there are plenty of other outfits who would give plenty to get a technical or business foothold in Kabulistan."

Provard was more upset than ever when informed about the theft of Tom's first drone plane model and the atomic explosion.

"That's why I preferred not to talk over the phone," the banker explained. "Since our enemy has agents right here in this country, I was afraid my line might be tapped."

It was now long past noon, and the banker accepted Tom's invitation to have lunch at Enterprises before flying back to New York. In spite of Chow's delicious food, everyone ate in glum silence.

"How come Ort Throme didn't fly with you?" Bud asked finally, trying to make conversation.

"He's off again on another painting trip," Provard replied. "This time to the South Seas."

A moment later the phone rang. Chow answered it, and said the call was for Mr. Provard. The banker, his face tense as if anticipating more bad news, lifted the receiver. As the others waited, they were astonished to see a happy grin spread over his face. Provard talked for five minutes, then hung up, smiling with relief.

"The most wonderful news!" he announced. "My office has just received another cable from Kabulistan. Schuyler Grane is safe! An Army patrol rescued him from three men who were taking him into the mountains!"

Bud gave a whoop and Tom himself, grinning at Ames, cheered inwardly.

"Two of the kidnapers," Provard went on, "were shot during the skirmish. The third is now a prisoner, but refuses to talk."

"What about the project, sir?" Tom pressed. "Are we in business again?"

The banker paused, glancing at Tom gravely. "I should say that's a question for you to answer, Tom. You and your crews are the ones who'll be exposed to any danger there may be."

"We'll risk it," Tom said, his blue eyes flashing. "The only assistants I'll take along will be volunteers."

Bud chuckled and raised his hand. "Sign me on as your first recruit, Sarge!"

Almost two weeks of frenzied preparation followed. A number of atomicars and trucks rolled off Ned Newton's assembly line at the Swift Construction Company. At the same time, skilled aircraft workers in another part of the plant were turning out a small fleet of magnetic homing pigeons powered by Tom's midget atomic power plants. Besides the mineral-detecting equipment and homing device, each plane was armed with the same simple "destroy" mechanism which Tom had installed in his successful second model.

Tom himself worked until late every evening, planning the almost endless details of the expedition—ordering and checking supplies, and laying out the work instructions for his carefully chosen volunteer crews. Only once were he and Bud able to slip away for a Saturday night date with the girls.

The following Monday morning, Mr. and Mrs. Swift, Sandy, Phyl, and her parents gathered on the Enterprises airfield to watch the expedition take off. Besides the *Sky Queen,* four huge cargo jets were lined up on the runways.

"Best of luck, son," Mr. Swift said, gripping Tom's hand warmly. "This is a magnificent project and I know you'll carry it through."

"Thanks, Dad. I'll do my best."

Mrs. Swift was misty-eyed as Tom embraced her. "I shan't worry," she told him, "but do come back as soon as you can, dear."

Sandy kissed her brother good-by, and Phyl shyly added a parting kiss on the cheek.

"How about me?" Bud grumbled, pretending to glower jealously.

"Right through that entrance hatch," Sandy replied with a giggle, pointing to the *Sky Queen*. Then she relented and gave him a hasty peck on the cheek, blushing as she did so.

Ed Longstreet, who had begged to come along on the expedition, thanked the Swifts for their hospitality. Harlan Ames, who was to handle security liaison with the Kabulistan government, shook hands with the Swifts and Newtons, as did Chow, before climbing aboard the Flying Lab.

Soon, the huge silver-winged sky giant roared aloft, followed in order by each of the cargo jets. Soon all were flying in graceful V-formation high over the Atlantic.

Late that afternoon, as the four jets proceeded across Iran to the camp site in Kabulistan, Tom landed at the Teheran airport. He and Ames had to make rail-shipping arrangements for later supplies. These would be sent overland from the Persian Gulf via the Trans-Iranian Railway.

Meanwhile, Ed and Bud started out by taxi for

the Teheran bazaar. "If I can find out where that
jeweler got the rubies, we may have a real clue
to the Amir's Mine," Ed said hopefully.

Bud was wide-eyed as he viewed the bustling
city of almost two million people. Like Shirabad,
Teheran was a city of contrasts. The streets
swarmed with vehicular traffic, yet sheep, goats,
and even camels plodded here and there among
the cars and buses. Many women still wore the
chadar—the native capelike costume.

The brick-arcaded bazaar was a maze of covered
streets stretching for miles. Its booths displayed
brassware, shoes, spices, perfume, food—hundreds
of different items.

"What? No Persian rugs?" Bud quipped.

"They're sold at the rug mart," Ed replied,
then suddenly pointed to a booth ahead. "There's
the fellow!"

A shaven-headed man stood behind a counter
laden with beads, bracelets, and other ornamen-
tal jewelry. At first he shrugged off Ed's questions
about the rubies. But when Ed took out a ten-
dollar bill, indicating he would make a purchase,
the man smiled slyly.

"Kheli khoob! Very good!" he murmured. "Return tonight, alone, and I shall take you to someone who knows where the rubies came from!"

CHAPTER XIV

FIERCE TRIBESMEN

ED Longstreet shot a triumphant glance at Bud. "What time shall I meet you?" he asked the jewelry shop owner.

"At the hour of sunset." The man salaamed.

"Hope the guy's on the level," Bud thought, after Ed bought a necklace and they left.

When Tom and Ames returned to the *Sky Queen* later that day, after making the rail-shipping arrangements, they found Bud and Ed waiting for them.

"I'm going to play detective," Ed announced.

When he reported the bargain he had made with the jeweler, both Tom and Ames, like Bud, were dubious about the deal.

"Maybe I'm being unduly suspicious," the security chief said with a frown, "but the whole thing sounds fishy to me. If there's any secret about the source of those rubies, the persons involved aren't likely to reveal it to a total stranger. For all they know, you might be a detective or police agent."

"I agree," Tom said. "This could be a trap."

Ed, however, was so eager to go ahead that Tom reluctantly gave his okay to the arrangement. But he insisted that precautions be taken.

"Suppose we set up a stakeout," Ames suggested. "The three of us will keep watch nearby when Ed meets this fellow, and then follow them."

"Good idea, I guess," Ed agreed.

All four taxied to the bazaar for a preliminary look at the scene of the rendezvous. Ed, an accomplished linguist who spoke Persian as well as several other languages, directed the driver to a certain public square which opened off from the bazaar.

"See that archway?" Bud said to Tom and Ames. He pointed to an opening in the arcade. "The jeweler's booth is just a little way inside, to the right."

Ed added, "The man and I will probably come out there."

Ames glanced about the square. Among the shops and buildings was an open-air restaurant.

"That'll make a perfect place for us to keep watch," Ames said. "The rest of us will be eating there when you go into the bazaar. Soon as you come out, we'll trail you."

"Right!" Ed agreed.

Shortly before seven o'clock, Tom, Bud, and Ames strolled casually back to the restaurant. They talked and joked like footsore tourists. As they sat down at a table, a waiter bustled up, salaamed, and took their orders.

Presently he returned with a plate of what looked like glistening black beads—caviar from the Caspian Sea. This was followed by bowls of *mast,* somewhat like cottage cheese. Then came a cucumber salad, flat disk-shaped "loaves" of bread, and generous servings of *tchelo-kebob.* This consisted of fluffy rice mixed with raw egg yolk and topped by strips of broiled lamb.

"Hmm! Not bad!" Bud said, sampling the dish.

As they ate, a taxi, which they had hired previously, drew up and parked at the curb nearby.

"There goes Ed!" Tom murmured when the trio started on dessert—a pastry stuffed with honey and chopped nuts.

His cousin was just walking into the covered bazaar. A minute later they saw him come out through the archway. At his side was the shaven-headed jeweler, now wearing a black skull cap. At a word from the jeweler, Ed beckoned a cab and the two climbed in.

Quickly Tom paid and tipped the waiter, as Ames murmured, "Let's go!" The trio hurried to their own waiting taxi.

Ed's cab was just disappearing down a street that led off from the square. At Ames's command, their driver sped away in pursuit.

By this time the sun had disappeared behind the city rooftops in a red glow. The cab ahead plunged into a heavy stream of traffic coursing down a broad avenue. As they followed, Tom caught passing glimpses of imposing government buildings, shops, a gorgeously domed mosque, and several tall, modernistic apartment buildings.

Leaving the center of the city behind, Ed's taxi entered a poorer section—an area of narrow, twisting streets and squalid, mud-brick buildings.

The deepening darkness helped to make the pursuit less noticeable. Presently the car ahead stopped, and Ames told their own driver to pull over.

Ed and the jeweler got out, paid their driver, and entered a drab, whitewashed building. Minutes passed, then half an hour, as Tom, Bud, and Ames waited anxiously. When an hour had gone by, the watchers became alarmed.

"We've waited long enough!" Tom said. "Let's investigate!"

The street was in a residential neighborhood, and the building into which Ed and the jeweler had gone seemed to be a beehive of separate living apartments. The three Americans knocked on several doors and tried to ask questions. But the occupants—swarthy men, and women with broods of ragged children—merely looked blank.

"It's hopeless. They don't understand English," Tom said tersely. "We'll have to call the police."

Ames and Bud remained on watch while Tom taxied to the nearest police station. Much time was wasted as he explained to the mustachioed official, Inspector Hassan, what had happened. Finally a police car was dispatched to the scene. The lawmen questioned numerous occupants of the building, but could learn nothing.

"This central hallway leads through to a back alley," Bud pointed out. "If that jeweler spotted us following him, he may have taken Ed through the building just to throw us off the track."

"I'm afraid Bud's right," Ames agreed.

After searching every room, the police gave up. Tom, Bud, and Ames accompanied them back to the station, where the inspector took notes; then the Americans taxied to the United States Embassy. The Embassy officials promised to do everything possible to press a search.

After a sleepless, worrisome night aboard the *Sky Queen,* Tom and his two companions hurried into the city to check back with the police and the Embassy. Neither had any news. An Embassy aide, however, said that the government had ordered a citywide dragnet to determine Ed's fate.

Meanwhile, the police had already checked the jeweler's booth at the bazaar. It was still closed. There was no clue to the man's whereabouts.

Tom passed the day restlessly with Bud, in a vain attempt to pick up a clue to the grave situation. In despair they did a little touring, visiting the Gulistan Palace with its famous jeweled Peacock Throne, the beautiful Sepah Salar Mosque, and also the House of Strength, a private gymnasium. Here, well-built, mustachioed muscle men swung heavy clubs and wrestled to rhythmic drumbeats and chanted verses.

"How'd you like to try a fall with one of those babies?" Bud whispered.

"No, thanks." Tom grinned wryly. "But I'll bet Chow could show 'em a few tricks, Texan-style."

Twenty-four hours later there was still no news of Ed. At the police station, Tom asked desperately when the dragnet could be expected to yield any results.

Inspector Hassan said he could not guess. "*Farda,*" he murmured. "Tomorrow, perhaps."

When Tom returned to the airport, he reached a hard decision. "I just can't wait any longer," he told Ames. "I'm needed on the project. Would you mind staying here alone to keep in touch with the situation?"

Ames squeezed his young friend's shoulder sympathetically. "Sure, skipper. You go on and try not to worry. I'll keep things buzzing here till Ed turns up."

Soon the *Sky Queen* was winging across trackless desert wastes, then over snow-capped highlands to Kabulistan. Tom bypassed the capital city of Shirabad and headed for the camp site.

"Hey! How about that?" Bud exclaimed as it loomed into view below.

The camp was humming with activity. Tents, metal shacks, and prefabricated warehouses had already been set up at the bend of the river. Bulldozers manned by native workmen were busily smoothing out an airfield.

The first to greet Tom and the others as they landed were Chow and Hank Sterling. "Nice going, Hank," Tom said to the husky blond engineer as they shook hands. "Looks as though you've really been busy."

"We'll be ready to start the mineral survey in two days," Hank reported.

Both he and the Texan were dismayed to hear of Ed's disappearance. "But never fear, buckaroo," Chow said to Tom. "I got a hunch he'll be okay."

Tom spent the rest of the afternoon and evening checking over every detail of the setup. After breakfast the next morning, Bud suggested they take an atomicar and explore the terrain.

The two boys started out across the valley

plain, then upward along slopes clad in a green-
ish-brown stubble of camel grass. As they traveled
higher, leaving the camp far behind, the uplands

became more fertile. Dense shrubbery and wooded patches appeared.

Suddenly the boys were startled by the sound of thundering hoofbeats. They gaped in surprise, as two fierce-looking hill tribesmen came gallop-

ing over the ridge on horseback. The turbaned, baggy-trousered riders were shouting and brandishing long glittering spears.

Tom's face tightened. "We'd better take to the air quick!"

He stabbed the repelatron button on the dashboard and the atomicar zoomed up and away in the nick of time, as the tribesmen hurled their spears upward. The well-aimed weapons only pinged against the underside of the car.

"Whew!" Bud muttered as the boys flew on. "Some reception!"

Tom felt a surge of worry at the evident hostility of the hard-riding mountaineers. Did this portend trouble for his base camp? Yet, from all accounts he had read of Kabulistan, the days when wild tribesmen raided innocent travelers were long past.

"Maybe they were just overly enthusiastic," Tom remarked hopefully.

"That kind of enthusiasm I can do without," Bud retorted. "Maybe those 'rumors' Simon Wayne told us about are true."

Presently, since there was no further sign of the attackers, Tom decided to land. He set the atomicar down gently on a level spot near a small blue lake.

"Are you game to explore a bit on foot?" Tom asked Bud.

"Sure! Looks like swell hiking country."

The two boys slid back the canopy and climbed out of the atomicar. They walked to the lake and began skirting the shore.

Bang! . . . Bang! . . . Bang!

To Tom and Bud's horror, a band of the same fierce-looking horsemen, this time armed with rifles, came charging out of a thick grove of poplars and mountain willows. Riding at a gallop, they gave the boys no chance to spring back to the car. Realizing they were trapped, both youths tried to keep a bold front.

"We're friends!" Tom cried, raising his voice. "Why attack—when we come in peace?"

His words were drowned by the furious shouts of the horsemen. Reining up sharply, they leaped from their saddles and swarmed about the two young Americans. In a few moments Tom's and Bud's hands were bound.

Then the bearded leader drew a curved, scimitarlike blade from his gaudy cummerbund. He brandished it menacingly at the boys.

Tom and Bud paled. "Looks as though he means business!" Bud gasped.

CHAPTER XV

NIGHT RAID

TOM and Bud silently uttered prayers as the Kabulistan chieftain, ranting at them loudly, flicked his scimitar closer to their faces.

Tom felt utterly helpless. Were he and Bud really about to be killed? Would he never see his mother and dad, or Sandy and Phyl again?

Suddenly a distant shout broke in on the chieftain's tirade. Tom and Bud stared. A horseman, wearing a sun helmet and khaki riding breeches, came galloping down the slope. Two other riders followed close behind. The boys' captors turned to face the newcomers.

The leading horseman was hawk-faced and black-bearded. Something about him seemed familiar. Suddenly Tom gasped. "Flambo!"

Bud scowled, half in rage and half in fear. "I told you that guy was our enemy!" he muttered.

"I'll bet he's the one who started these hot-shots gunning for us!"

Flambo reined in his horse with a splatter of dust and gravel, then sprang to the ground. He barked something at the chieftain in a guttural tongue. Soon all the tribesmen were chattering back at him. They gesticulated wildly, first at the two boys, then toward the atomicar.

"*Kefaya!*" Flambo waved his hand to quiet them. Then he said to the two boys, "You have been most unwise."

"You mean coming here unarmed?" Tom retorted. "We've done nothing. Why should your men attack us?"

The swarthy engineer frowned. "These are not my people. They are Baluchi tribesmen—somewhat wild, as you see, but perfectly willing to be friends. Unfortunately, at their first approach, you frightened them out of their wits by zooming off in your flying car."

The tribesmen, Flambo went on, had concluded the car was bewitched, and that its riders must be in league with Shaitan.

"What did they expect us to do?" Bud growled. "The way those spearmen came whooping down on us didn't look like any game of tag. A fine way to make friends!"

Flambo chuckled, showing his white even teeth. "A bit terrifying, no doubt. You see, the moun-

tain tribes in this part of the world have always
been free as hawks. Next to his horse, a spear or
a rifle is a man's best friend—and he is apt to use
it out of sheer high spirits."

"We've come here to help them keep their freedom," Tom said.

Flambo eyed the young inventor keenly, then
murmured, "Yes, I think I believe you."

He turned and spoke to the tribesmen for a
few minutes. Their leathery, sunburned faces
gradually broke into friendly grins. At a word
from their chief, two of them untied Tom and
Bud.

"This is Fazir Khan," Flambo said, introduc-
ing their leader.

The Khan laughed, slapped the boys on the
back, and pumped their hands in a sinewy grip.
As he did so, he poured out a flood of words.

"He is inviting us all to be his guests," Flambo
translated. He added dryly, "I think it would be
wise to accept."

Tom smiled. "We'll be honored."

The boys were allowed to go in the atomicar.
The tribesmen eyed it suspiciously at first. But
seeing that Tom and Bud made no effort to fly
off, the men were soon riding alongside, cheering
and playfully firing off their rifles into the air.

The triumphal procession proceeded to the
Baluchi camp, several miles away. Veiled women
and bright-eyed children came from their tents to

stare at the strangers. Many wore bangles and ear-rings.

In the gaily carpeted chieftain's tent, huge sil-ver samovars were brought out and the guests were served tea. Then later came a huge feast. The main course was roasted sheep's head. The meal ended with melons, figs, and pomegranates for dessert.

Fazir Khan made a long speech of welcome. Tom replied, with Flambo acting as interpreter. Then the Khan presented each boy with a curv-ing, intricately carved sword of Damascus steel. They acknowledged the gifts with gestures and smiles.

"What can *we* give, skipper?" Bud wondered.

"Our wrist watches," Tom whispered.

The Khan and his wife were delighted with these tokens.

"Now they'll be able to sneak past your alarm system," Bud said to Tom with a chuckle.

The Swift home at Shopton was protected by an electromagnetic field. The family and all their close friends wore wrist watches containing tiny neutralizer coils to keep the person approaching from setting off the electronic alarm.

Tom now invited their hosts to come for a ride in the atomicar. At first only the Khan was brave enough to try. He howled with glee as the car soared and hedgehopped. Then all the tribesmen clamored for a ride. At last the two young

Americans were allowed to depart. Flambo and his men accompanied them part way back to the base camp.

Tom felt sure that Flambo was not the enemy behind all their troubles. Before leaving the Middle Easterner, Tom decided to ask him about the secret Assassins cult which Simon Wayne had mentioned.

Flambo scoffed. "Your friend Wayne has his geography a trifle mixed up. The cult never centered here in Kabulistan. Their stronghold was the Rock of Alamut in the Elburz Mountains of northern Persia."

Tom felt relieved. "Thanks," he said to Flambo as they shook hands. "You've not only saved our lives—you've also taken a load off my mind."

At sundown, the valley in which the base camp was located soon cooled off from the day's heat. A bracing breeze blew down from the mountain peaks. Darkness came fast, and the night sky was studded with stars.

Some time after midnight, Tom was awakened by a disturbance outside the camp. He jumped from his bunk, pulled on khaki slacks, and stepped into his loafers. Then he pressed a switch and hurried outdoors. Bud followed sleepily.

The switch had turned on a series of floodlights which ringed the camp. In the bright glare crewmen and hired native workers could be seen rushing out of their shacks and tents.

"Raiders!" Bud gasped, snapping wide awake.

A clatter of hoofbeats echoed back as several fleeing horsemen galloped away into the darkness.

"Brand my runnin' iron, them rustlers ain't gonna get away from a Texas cowboy!" Chow bellowed.

The doughty Texan made a rush for his own mount. This was a beautiful Arab mare which Chow had bought from a passing band of tribesmen.

In seconds he had the sleek, dapple-gray horse bridled. Without waiting to saddle her, Chow snatched up a coil of rope and took off.

Tom and the others were so startled they could only gape. The cook raced out of camp with a volley of wild Indian war whoops.

"Chow! Wait!" Tom yelled, finding his voice. "They may be armed!"

He and Bud were about to follow in an atomicar when Chow returned, beaming proudly. He was leading a prisoner, bound with his lariat.

"Well done, pardner!" Tom said.

He summoned Ali, the interpreter Hank had used in hiring workmen. The captive, a turbaned mountaineer, listened sullenly to Ali's questions. But his only reply was a shake of the head and a few muttered words.

Ali turned to Tom and shrugged. "I can get nothing out of him."

Puzzled and uneasy, Tom gave orders for the prisoner to be placed under guard. He also detailed several of his American crewmen to act as sentries for the rest of the night. The camp finally settled back to sleep.

The next morning, as Tom was finishing breakfast in the mess hall, Hank walked in. His square-jawed face had a grim look.

"What's up?" Tom asked.

"Our native workmen won't finish the airstrip," Hank said. "They want their wages."

Tom hurried outside. The men were standing around in tense little groups. They looked fearful.

"What's this all about, Ali?" Tom said.

The interpreter fidgeted and gave an evasive reply. Tom tried to question him but got nowhere. Finally he called for the prisoner to be brought out. One look at his sly grin gave Tom a clue.

"So he's been talking, has he?" Tom snapped at Ali. "What were he and his friends up to last night? Or would you rather tell the police?"

Ali's eyes widened worriedly. "Okay, sir. I tell you," the interpreter gulped. "The men who came last night planted land mines all about the camp. Who knows where? Anyone who steps in the wrong spot may be blown to pieces!"

CHAPTER XVI

A TERRIFIED CAMP

LAND mines! Tom and Hank stared at each other in dismay.

Most of the other Swift crewmen and technicians had gathered to watch Tom quiz Ali and the prisoner. A few of them tried to wisecrack to hide their uneasiness. But others, especially the men who had families back in Shopton, looked frankly worried.

"Where were the mines planted?" Tom asked. "On the airfield?"

Ali shook his head stubbornly. "No, sir. I tell you truly just what he say. He and the other bad men bury mines all over, even here among our tents and huts. Maybe one minute from now someone walks on one. Then *boom!*" The interpreter flung his hands wide, his eyes blazing.

"They didn't have time to mine the whole camp!" Hank argued.

"How do we know?" spoke up Les Nixon, a young geologist. "They could have been digging away like moles for a couple of hours before we got wise to 'em!"

The prisoner chuckled, evidently enjoying the Americans' distress. This was too much for one crewman.

"I'll wipe off that grin, you sneaking rat!" he growled. Before Tom could stop him, he lashed out a fast uppercut that knocked the captive head over heels.

"Cut it out!" Tom snapped, grabbing the crewman's arm and jerking him away from the cowering prisoner. "That's not going to help any!"

"Then tell us what is!" someone else retorted. "I sure don't want to be the guy who steps on the first of those mines!"

"First, second, what does it matter?" put in a mechanic named Deever. "Even one's too dog-gone many for comfort if we don't know where it's planted!"

Deever's words were backed up with a murmur of agreement. Seeing the Americans' worried re-actions, the hired workmen began to chatter, and pleaded loudly to be paid off at once.

"Quiet! *Everyone!*" Tom shouted. Turning to

Ali, he said, "Tell them they have nothing to worry about. I'll check over the whole camp myself and clear out every single mine—if there really are any. In the meantime, warn them to stay right where they are!"

Bud grinned and muttered to Chow, "Smart move, eh? They stay put for their own safety—which means they *can't* quit."

"Mebbe so, but how about Tom?" the loyal cook replied worriedly.

"What're you going to do, skipper?" asked Les.

"You've heard of mine detectors, haven't you?" Tom countered.

"Have we got one?"

"If not, I'll make one."

Finding none on the *Sky Queen,* Tom hurried to his laboratory and quickly rigged up a simple, but highly sensitive, detection circuit. He fitted it into a flat plastic case and jointed on a length of rigid tubing—thus making a long-handled pancake probe. To this, he wired a set of earphones.

When he emerged from the Flying Lab, Tom strode to the prisoner and jerked him to his feet. Then he turned to Ali. "Tell this guy he's coming along with me while I pry out those mines."

Ali flashed a wicked smile. "Most excellent justice, sir!"

As he translated Tom's words, the prisoner began to tremble and protest fearfully.

"Get that sword Fazir Khan gave me," Tom said to Bud.

His chum grinned, darted off to their hut, and returned a moment later, fingering the edge of the razor-sharp blade.

"Tell the prisoner he'll push the stick along and I'll wear the earphones. Bud will carry this sword which will be tickling the man's neck in case he tries any fast moves."

Ali was beside himself with glee as he translated. The American crewmen and hired workmen looked on appreciatively. Side by side with his unwilling helper, Tom began the slow process of probing the camp grounds and the nearly completed airfield. In twenty minutes he heard the first buzz over his earphones.

Slowly and cautiously Tom scratched away the earth with a stick as everyone watched in breathless silence. The prisoner's eyes were glassy with fear, but Bud stood by with the sword to prevent a break for freedom.

Presently the hidden mine came into view. Tom whistled and murmured to his chum. "This is no amateur job, Bud!"

Guided by his keen scientific intuition, Tom deactivated the ugly device. But he could feel the cold drops of perspiration trickling down his back as he did so.

"Whew!" Bud gasped. "If I hadn't known what

a scientific whiz you are, pal, I'd be a quivering mass of jelly by now!"

Hours went by with agonizing slowness as Tom probed the base foot by foot. Five other mines were uncovered and disarmed. Tom was able to speed up the job somewhat by watching the prisoner's behavior. Whenever they neared a danger spot, the man's nervousness increased. In safe areas, he was noticeably calm.

At last, by midafternoon, Tom felt that the job was finished. He called Ali and grilled the prisoner. Rolling his eyes, the fellow swore fervently that every mine which the raiders had buried was now uncovered.

"Okay, fellows!" Tom shouted. "I guess it's all clear!"

The camp broke into thunderous cheers, and the faces of the workmen were wreathed in smiles of relief. Chow, who had confidently gone off to his cookshack to start dinner, emerged clutching a heavy skillet.

"Yip-pee!" The stout old cook ripped off his chef's hat and let out a Texas bronc-buster's whoop. In his excitement he even hurled the skillet through the air. It landed in a patch of brush, just beyond the edge of camp.

BO-O-OOM! The ground shook beneath his feet, as hunks of earth and stones exploded through the air and showered down in all directions. When the dust finally cleared, the patch of brush was now a gaping hole, ten feet wide.

"Chow! For Pete's sake, are you all right?"

Bud and half a dozen other crewmen came runing over to the chef. The roly-poly Texan was still dazed and speechless with shock.

"B-b-brand my poached egg!" Chow stuttered. "Am I all in one piece?"

"Yes, and your bay window's as big as ever," Bud told him. "But you're about ten shades whiter than dough!"

Tom had instinctively grabbed the prisoner to keep him from escaping. The young inventor's blue eyes blazed with fury, and his fingers tightened like a steel vise on the terrified captive.

"So every last mine's been uncovered, has it?" The man cowered and trembled at Tom's ripsaw tone, even though not understanding a word. Tom decided to try a ruse to get the truth. "Ali, tell this rat I'm going to reactivate one of those mines and then drag him over it at the end of a rope!"

As Ali translated, the man fell to his knees, his face ashen. He clasped the front of Tom's shirt and began to blubber out a plea for mercy.

Tom's face was hard as rock. "Was that the last mine?"

"He says No," Ali translated. "There is one more—near the river where the men go to bathe."

"Fine," Tom said coldly. "He can show me where and help dig it out."

When this mine had been uncovered and de-activated, the prisoner vowed that no more had been planted. He was shaking with fear at the menacing expressions of the Americans and native workmen. Several of the latter had taken out knives and were whetting them with meaningful glances at the captive.

Tom felt that the man might now be willing to talk more freely. Through Ali, he pressed him with questions. But the captive swore he had no idea who was behind the mine planting. He himself had been hired by another group of raiders. Tom was convinced the man was telling the truth, but took no chances.

"Tell him we'll keep him here as a hostage as long as the camp's in operation," Tom said to Ali. "If another mine explodes, I'll turn him over to the workmen for quick justice."

After translating, Ali grinned. "Sir, I think we need fear no more mines," he reported.

As the next two days went by, the base took on the look of a busy settled community. Workshops, laboratories, and repair hangars were quickly erected. A convoy of atomicars and trucks was sent out, headed by two Swift hydraulic engineers and a professor from Grandyke University, near Shopton, who had just arrived by jet. They were to plan an irrigation system for the whole country, so drought-parched lands could be watered for future farming.

On the third day after the land-mine scare, the first fleet of drone magnetic homing pigeons was launched. Several were fitted with cameras for aerial mapping. Two cartographers from the U. S. Coast and Geodetic Survey had flown in and would provide Kabulistan with its first accurate maps.

"I should be getting reports on the drones soon," Tom thought eagerly. "I hope they're encouraging."

Two of the drones beeped on the first flight out. When the sites were checked later, one proved to be a low-grade iron ore deposit, the other of zinc. A third plane, which beeped the following day, failed to come back to base.

"It must have crashed, skipper," George Dilling reported gloomily.

Tom studied the chart of its flight area in the communications shack. "Where, approximately, would the bird have been when it beeped?" he asked.

Dilling fingered the spot on the map. He had already figured the position by computer.

"Okay, we'll trace its whole flight course between there and camp," Tom said.

He and Bud took off at once in a Whirling Duck. The drone had been flying a gridlike search pattern to the northeast. Hours went by with no sight of the lost homing pigeon. Finally the boys found themselves over a secluded mountain valley.

"We must be coming close to the spot where —" Tom stopped speaking.

A sudden blast of ack-ack fire had thundered from the valley. "We've been hit!" he cried.

CHAPTER XVII

THE AMIR'S MINE

THE attack on the helijet had come with such stunning suddenness that neither Tom nor Bud knew what to expect next.

But now Bud cried out, "Down there! Look!"

A slim, deadly-looking antiaircraft gun was poking up from the brush-covered floor of the valley. It wheeled, keeping the muzzle trained on the helijet. But there was no further fire. The first burst had done its job.

"The controls won't answer!" Tom said, working the stick desperately.

Part of the fuselage had been shattered, and one wing almost shot away. The craft was yawing and swooping crazily.

Bud gulped. "What about the rotor?"

Tom had already thumbed the switch for this, and the blades were now knifing out into flight position. But the pulse jets coughed and died, after giving the rotor a quick spin.

"Oh—oh! The fuel line must have been hit!" Bud's face was pale as he added, "Radio's conked out, too!"

"We'll have to land," Tom said.

The slowly whirling rotor eased the descent as they sank helplessly toward the valley floor. After long moments, the boys touched down to a bumpy landing.

"Still in one piece, anyhow," Tom muttered.

"So far. But what about those jokers who winged us?"

The boys climbed out and hastily scanned the valley. "We must be a mile from the ack-ack gun placement," Tom told Bud. "Come on! Let's scram before they send out a mop-up squad!"

The two youths took off at a sprint, heading for the nearest slope.

"Plenty of timber up there!" Tom said on the run. "If we can reach higher ground, at least we'll be able to find cover!"

They had gone scarcely a hundred yards when a rifleshot cracked on their right. The shell ricocheted from a boulder just ahead with a loud whine! The boys stopped short with white faces.

"Don't move!" barked a voice. "And put up your hands!"

As the boys obeyed, a man stepped into view, his finger on the trigger of a powerful-looking military rifle. In appearance he might have been an American construction worker, but his guttural accent sounded Central European. Two hard-bitten mountain tribesmen were with him.

"Who are you?" Tom demanded boldly. "If you had anything to do with shooting down our plane, I warn you—"

"Shut up!" the man growled, then broke into a harsh, sneering laugh. "So *you* are warning *me*, eh? Ha—ha! A very good joke indeed!"

His laughter died away abruptly as he snapped out orders to the two tribesmen. In seconds the boys' hands were tied behind them. Then they were marched along the valley at gun point, back toward the ack-ack placement.

At last their captor gave the order to halt. He jerked up his rifle and fired a shot into the air. In response, a clump of brush seemed to raise itself from the ground!

Tom and Bud gasped. The brush was used to hide a trap door in the ground. From it led a flight of metal stairs.

"Down with you!" the rifleman said.

The boys descended cautiously. The steepness of the ladderlike stairway was unnerving, especially since their hands were tied.

About twenty feet below, the shaft opened into a lighted tunnel. The man with the rifle prodded Tom and Bud along with his gun. The tunnel was dirt-floored, its walls shored with moldy ancient timbers. The timbering had been reinforced with new-looking metal beams.

Presently the tunnel ended in a door. Their captor gave a shout. Instantly the door swung open, as if at the press of a button.

"Ah! Welcome, my friends!" boomed a hearty voice.

Tom and Bud gaped in stunned surprise. The speaker was a huge, bear-sized man who was seated at a desk. An enormous blond handlebar mustache jutted out on each side of his ruddy-cheeked face.

"*Simon Wayne!*" Tom cried out.

"Exactly. Come in and take a load off your feet, boys!" Wayne invited, waving toward chairs. "I recognized you via a hidden television eye just outside the trap door. A jolly surprise, eh?"

Simon Wayne roared with laughter. "You'll have to admit, son, it's an original way to bag guests—with an antiaircraft gun!"

"I suppose you also shot down our missing drone?" Tom said.

Wayne nodded. "Yes, indeed. I've been trying hard to lay hands on one of your atomic capsules so I could copy the design. Never expected one would come flying right into my web!"

As Wayne chuckled, Tom and Bud glanced at each other with a look of furious understanding.

"So you're the sneak who buzzed the *Sky Queen* on the flight back from New Mexico!"

Bud accused. "And hijacked the first drone plane too, I'll bet!"

"Certain employees of mine did, acting on my orders," Wayne admitted.

A sudden suspicion flared in Tom's mind as he recalled the blast that had shattered the building in which the stolen magnetic homing pigeon had been hidden. One of the two victims had been Mr. Goldtooth—which meant that Simon Wayne was also involved in the ruby mine mystery!

"What *is* this underground hideout of yours, Wayne?" Tom demanded.

The beefy sales-engineer grinned. "You've guessed, eh? Well, you're quite right, my dear Swift. You are now inside the *Amir's Mine!*"

As Bud gasped, Wayne reached into a drawer of his desk and took out a handful of yellowing printed pages. "Perhaps you found what was left of that book, *Travels in Remotest Araby*. These are the torn-out pages."

"Is that how you found the mine?" Bud asked.

Wayne shook his head. "Not at all. I was simply making sure no one else would find it. You see," Wayne went on, after pausing to light a cigar, "I stumbled on these old mine workings months ago. That was when Europa Fabrik first sent me to Kabulistan to wangle a development contract. Needless to say, I kept my discovery secret—even from my own company."

Later, Wayne explained, he had returned to the United States, and tried to buy the patent rights to Tom Swift's midget power plant. This, he felt, would help convince the Shah that Europa Fabrik should be given a free hand in developing Kabulistan's resources.

"Naturally I would have been in charge of the project," Wayne added with a sly chuckle. "A perfect chance to work the mine secretly—and make myself rich beyond belief!"

He opened another drawer and took out several glinting red gems.

"Just look at these rubies!" Wayne gloated. "Do you realize this mine is worth millions? But you, Tom my boy, ruined my plan with your stubbornness. And your friend Provard copped the contract, instead of Europa Fabrik. Even so, I think I'll be able to snatch quite a fortune out of these mine workings before anyone finds out what's going on!"

To keep the local mountaineers away from the site, Wayne went on, he had hired several fake religious mullahs. On his orders, they had revived and spread the old stories about the mine being accursed by Shaitan.

"Clever, don't you think?" Wayne smirked and puffed his cigar. "Even that fellow Flambo's secretary fell for their superstitious tripe! But why sit here talking? I have a job for you, Swift."

Summoning the armed guard, whose name was Gursk, Wayne took the boys through several connecting mine tunnels.

"The workings extend for miles, like a rabbit warren, all through the valley," Wayne explained. "That's how Gursk was able to pop up from nowhere and capture you."

Besides Gursk, who kept his rifle aimed at their backs, Tom counted more than a dozen other men. Three of these, dressed in rumpled khaki shirts and shorts, seemed to be Europeans like Gursk. All were heavily armed. The others were whiskery, tough-looking mountaineers engaged in the actual work of ruby mining.

In a steel-walled chamber, Wayne showed the boys the ack-ack gun. Its telescoping mount enabled it to be drawn back underground.

At a number of points, the tunneling was pierced by vertical shafts leading up to ground level. These provided air and some light. "Of course the openings are camouflaged with brush and shrubbery," Wayne told Tom and Bud.

At last they came to a heavy steel door. Wayne unbolted it and gestured the two boys inside. Tom's eyes widened as he entered a large room. It was a scientific laboratory, crammed with the very latest research equipment!

The walls were lined with shelves of chemicals, electronic gear, handbooks and scientific journals, spectroscopic and X-ray devices, even an electron microscope. There were also machine tools, an electric furnace, and racks of hardware and metal stock, as well as a generator.

"Quite a layout, eh?" Wayne boasted.

Bud gave an angry cry and pointed to a far corner of the huge lab. On the floor lay the fuselage of the shot-down magnetic homing pigeon, partly disassembled.

"Pretty smart, that little sabotage device you put in," Wayne said to Tom. "It fouled up the atomic power plant just enough to destroy your secret magnetic-field controls for the plasma." Wayne chuckled. "But this time we won't have to risk another explosion, trying to figure out how it works."

"Meaning what?" Tom asked coolly.

"Meaning now we have the inventor himself— you—and *you're* going to put it back in perfect working order!"

"And suppose I refuse?"

Wayne's blue eyes hardened. "I wouldn't if I were you. Not if you and your chum hope to get out of here alive." He paused and bit off the tip of a fresh cigar. "When your midget atomic power plant's working again and you've filled me in on all the details, maybe we can make a deal. Until then, you'll both stay locked in here."

Wayne and Gursk moved toward the door. "That shaft leads up to ground level, by the way," Wayne added, pointing to an opening in the roof.

"But don't get any ideas. The outlet topside will be guarded night and day!"

As the steel door slammed behind them and the bolts shot into place, Bud slumped in despair.

"We're trapped, skipper!"

Tom's brain was already working at top speed. "That's what *they* think!" he retorted grimly.

Back at the base camp, as afternoon wore into evening, Dilling, Hank, and the others tried repeatedly to make radio contact with the two boys. Darkness fell, with still no report. Hank took the *Sky Queen* out on a hasty search, but was forced to give up.

"It's hopeless. We'll just have to wait for daylight," he told his companions.

The whole camp was plunged into gloom by the disappearance of Tom and Bud. Half the night had gone by when a sentry yanked the alarm siren. Floodlights blazed across the camp and crewmen tumbled out of their bunks.

"What's up?" Hank Sterling came charging out of his shack on the double.

The sentry ran to meet him. "Horsemen!" he shouted. "We're being attacked!"

CHAPTER XVIII

SURPRISE BLAST-OFF

A DRUM of hoofbeats could be heard thundering toward the camp. The riders were still beyond view because of the darkness, but were drawing closer by the second.

Hank barked out orders. "Arv, get the tear-gas guns! Chow, start issuing gas masks!"

Hank and his men had only moments to rally their defenses before the horsemen came galloping across the airfield into camp. The two in front were wearing khaki field garb. The others—all brandishing rifles—were either wearing high-flapped felt hats, or the turbans of the Baluchi tribesmen.

"Hold it!" shouted Hank.

His iron-voiced command brought the horsemen to a clattering halt as they reined in sharply. All were streaked with dust and looked as if they had ridden hard and far.

"Put away that weapon!" the black-bearded leader snapped. "We come as friends!"

Hank's eyes narrowed as he recognized Nurhan Flambo.

"We'll lower our shootin' irons when your hombres drop them rifles!" Chow growled.

"Don't be foolish," Flambo said. "We are not rustlers from your Wild West!" Nevertheless, he gave an order to the tribesmen.

Scowling, they slipped the rifles into their saddle sheaths.

"Pretty late at night, isn't it, for a friendly visit?" Hank said evenly.

"Not if the mission is urgent," Flambo said. "One of your aircraft has failed to return, has it not?"

The Americans stiffened, tense and eager, but fearing bad news.

"That's right," Hank said. "Do you know anything about it?"

"It crashed over a mountain valley, somewhere northeast of here."

Flambo's words drew gasps of dismay. He explained that he had received the news several hours before when he had stopped at a village. The message had been passed along by signals and couriers.

"You mean you got spies all over these tarnation mountains?" Chow blurted out suspiciously.

Flambo smiled. "Let us say, sources of information. My company *belongs* here in the Middle East, you see," he said pointedly. "We still hope to undertake one or two projects for the Kabulistan government."

"Brand my coyote cookies, then your hombres musta been the ones who spied on Tom and Bud an' me when we first camped here!" Chow said. "An' shot off that signal flare, too!"

The black-bearded engineer showed his teeth in a flickering grin. "Would *you* not keep a sharp lookout if a rival rancher sent his herd to graze on *your* range?"

Chow's shrewdly squinting eyes met Flambo's. In spite of himself, the leathery old Texan could not repress a chuckle. "Reckon I take your meanin', pardner!"

"Listen!" Hank broke in. "It's Tom and Bud we're worrying about right now. Can you tell us exactly where the crash occurred?"

Flambo shook his head. "Unfortunately, no. But I can take you to the man who saw it and first sent out the report. He's one of a band of Kurdish nomads living in the mountains far to the northeast. The quickest way to reach him would be by plane."

Arv, Slim Davis, and several other crewmen were still inclined to be suspicious of Flambo.

"How do we know we can trust him?" Arv demanded of Hank. "It might even be some kind of trap. Don't forget that phony tip to the Army colonel—or those land mines, either!"

Flambo, when questioned, angrily denied having any part in either incident. Hank and Chow both felt he was telling the truth.

"Okay, so we can't be sure," Hank admitted later as the Americans held a private council of war. "But he saved Tom and Bud from those wild tribesmen, didn't he? I think his offer of help is on the level."

The others, who were as anxious as Hank about the boys' fate, were convinced by this argument. At dawn Hank took off with Flambo in a cargo jet, leaving Arv in charge of the base.

Flambo, an amateur pilot himself, guided Hank to the site of the Kurdish encampment. But as they hovered down on their jet lifters, Hank saw that the hillside was deserted! Only the ashes of cooking fires and ground trampled by livestock showed where the camp had been.

"What is this? A trick?" Hank snapped.

Flambo's face darkened. "I do not deal in tricks," he said. "As I told you, these people are nomads—wandering herdsmen. Quite plainly, they have moved on."

Reviving his hopes, Hank began scouting around by air. The nomads certainly could not have traveled far in one day. Half an hour later, as the plane winged over the hills, Flambo pointed to a rugged upland pasture on the right.

"Look! I can see them!" he exclaimed. "Down there is the new camp."

Hank swooped toward the spot. Tents dotted the steep hillside, with horses and camels tethered nearby. A few goats mingled with the flock of fat-tailed Karakul sheep that spread out over the slope.

As the jet descended, the nomads swarmed from their tents, shouting and firing their rifles. Even Flambo was surprised by their evident unfriendliness. Hank was more alarmed by the lack of level ground.

Beads of perspiration flicked out on his forehead as he made several attempts to set the big cargo jet down on the rugged slope. At last he gave up and zoomed skyward again.

"No use," Hank said.

Reluctantly he decided it would be wiser to fly back to camp and return in an atomicar. Hank was feverish with impatience at this new setback. Hours would be lost, since the atomicar's top speed was nowhere near that of the cargo jet.

It was midafternoon when they finally arrived back at the nomad camp. Again the natives tried to discourage a landing by shooting their rifles in the air. But Hank and Flambo landed safely. The nomads quieted somewhat and gathered around the car as Flambo spoke to them in Kurdish. Hank noticed the men wore fringed turbans—

the fringe serving to whisk away flies that buzzed about in the blistering sunlight.

Flambo spoke with them for several minutes. Then he turned to Hank with a puzzled look. "They are frightened of something," he reported.

"Of the flying car?"

"No, although they were a bit scared of that at first. Oddly enough, it seems to have something to do with that famous lost ruby mine."

Hank scoffed impatiently. "You mean just because it's supposed to be accursed by Shaitan?"

The effect of Hank's words was startling! The tribesmen cowered back, making superstitious gestures to ward off evil, their eyes blazing with fear.

"A bad mistake," Flambo scolded. "These are Yezidi Kurds—very shy and superstitious. They are so afraid of the devil they will not even pronounce his name."

Flambo singled out his own acquaintance, the man who had sent news of the crash, so he could speak to him alone. But the fellow shrank back fearfully and refused to reply.

Flambo repeated his questions, first pleading, then angry. He and Hank both emptied their pockets, hoping to tempt the nomad with money or gifts. But the man would say nothing.

Flambo sighed and gave up with a shrug. "It is hopeless. He probably is afraid to talk for fear his fellow tribesmen would kill him."

"Won't he even point out the direction of the plane crash?" Hank asked in exasperation.

Flambo shook his head. "It happened over the valley of the cursed ruby mine. But where that is—who can tell?"

At that very moment, in the underground mine laboratory, Tom Swift was about to carry out a daring plan. He had obeyed Simon Wayne's orders and set about putting his midget atomic power plant back in working order.

Wayne had dropped into the lab early that morning to check on his progress. The beefy engineer grinned smugly and twirled his mustache when he saw Tom busily at work.

"I knew you were smart, Swift!" Wayne said. "Play along with me and I may even cut you in on my ruby setup!"

He left, promising to return that afternoon. The minute Wayne bolted the door, Bud took out a small rocket fuselage which he had hastily shoved under the workbench.

"Good thing he doesn't suspect just *how* smart you are, skipper!" Bud said with a chuckle. He and Tom had been working frantically on the rocket all night long.

Hours later the rocket was completed. Tom quickly installed the atomic capsule and magnetic homing device inside. The memory drum was switched into "playback" circuit, and the master steering unit of the homing device was con-

The roar of Tom's message rocket shook
the whole mine

nected to small servo controls. These would operate the steering jets of the miniature rocket.

"How about the note?" Bud said.

"Coming right up." Tom hastily scribbled a note describing the method to be used in following the drone back to the mine. Then he screwed on the cover plate and the two boys mounted the rocket in a jerry-rigged launching rack. "Okay, Bud. Blast off!"

Bud pressed a switch button at the end of a cable.

Vroom! The rocket shot up the air shaft with a roar that shook the whole mine.

Angry shouts and cries followed. In a few seconds Wayne, Gursk, and two other armed men came bursting into the laboratory.

"Tough luck," Tom greeted them apologetically. "This dumb pal of mine just ran the atomic pack at too high amperage and it blew up." He waved at the evidence of an accidental blast which the boys had faked beforehand.

Wayne was red-faced with rage. As he calmed, a cruel glint came into his eye. "All right, Swift, you've outsmarted me this time. But no more. I have someone here who'll help us make sure that you do just what I say from now on!"

CHAPTER XIX

THE RUBY WEAPON

THERE was a cold ruthlessness in Wayne's tone that chilled Tom and Bud. The boys looked at each other uneasily. Who was the "someone" Wayne had referred to?

The hulking blond-mustachioed engineer turned to Gursk. He muttered an order in some European language. Gursk grinned and hurried off.

Tom and Bud waited tensely. Meanwhile, Wayne struck a match, lit a cigar, and eyed them with a malicious smile. Soon they heard footsteps coming back through the tunnel. Gursk prodded another man into the laboratory with his rifle—a thin young man in rumpled clothes with his hands tied behind his back.

"*Ed!*" Tom and Bud gasped out the name of Tom's cousin together.

"Another gullible fool who blundered right

into our hands!" Wayne chuckled, enjoying the two youths' discomfiture. Ed was as dismayed at finding Tom and Bud prisoners as they were at seeing him a captive, although the boys were thankful that he seemed to be unharmed.

Wayne smirked as he related the story behind Ed's capture. "The rubies from the mine," he said, "are being sold through various agents—one being the jeweler at the Teheran bazaar." Another was the bookseller in Shirabad. But all buyers were cautiously watched to keep the secret of the mine from leaking out. This vigilance covered also the fearful bookseller in Shirabad.

It had been Ed's questions to the jeweler about the rubies which had caused the gang to have him shadowed. This was done by "Mr. Goldtooth."

He had overheard Ed's chat with Provard about Tom Swift. Goldtooth had also learned that Ed was taking the gems to a London jewel expert for mounting. Later, in London, Ed was watched as he ransacked bookshops for old volumes on Kabulistan. When the spy reported his purchase of *Travels in Remotest Araby,* the gang became fearful that he, or Tom Swift, might pry out the secret of the mine—especially when Ed flew straight to Shopton. Since he had taken off before they had a chance to stop him, Goldtooth had caused the airport bomb scare to give him a chance to steal the book from Ed's luggage.

"Yes, indeed, you put us to a lot of trouble, Longstreet," Wayne said. "So you can imagine the laugh we got when you walked right into our clutches—practically the minute you landed in Teheran!"

Wayne slapped his thigh and roared with laughter. The three prisoners gave him cold looks of disgust. Wayne added to Tom and Bud, "You two gave me a laugh, the way you swallowed that yarn about the Assassins cult!"

Bud's eyes blazed with fury. "I suppose those land mines, and the phony tip that we were spies had you in stitches, too!"

Wayne nodded, still chuckling. "Quite right, my boy. Those were two more of my little jokes."

"Was Mirza Maruk one of your gang?" Tom questioned.

The boys' captor guffawed. "That useless fanatic! No. He was strictly a lone wolf!"

"So you've had your laugh," Tom said curtly. "What happens now?"

Wayne's face froze to a cruel mask as his eyes fastened on the young inventor. "I gave you a chance to play ball with us, Swift. Even offered to cut you in on the ruby mine! But you pulled a fast one. Now things will be rougher for you."

Wayne took out a watch and laid it on the laboratory workbench. "You have until eight tomorrow morning to write down the secret data and formulas for all major Swift inventions—including your midget atomic power plant. If you don't, both your cousin and your pal will be shot!" Gursk clicked the bolt of his rifle significantly.

"Just a little reminder," Wayne said. "This time I mean business!" He got up and left the lab. Gursk followed.

As the steel door clanged shut, the three prisoners looked at one another. All were pale. Tom and Bud quickly untied Ed's wrists and told him in low voices about the rocket.

"Supposing your plan works, Tom," Ed murmured. "Can the crew from the base get here before eight o'clock?"

"Easily, I should think," Tom said. "Unless they go to Shirabad first, to get help from the police or the Army."

Bud gave a worried whistle. "Boy! I never thought of that, skipper. They'll *have* to have help, won't they, if we hope to get out of here alive?"

"Can't you stall Wayne off somehow?" Ed put in. "I mean, write down a bunch of fake formulas."

Tom shrugged. "It's worth a try. But frankly I doubt if Wayne would be fooled. That guy's a top-flight engineer!"

"Then why not give him the real stuff?" Bud suggested. "We can make sure it'll never do him any good, once we get out of here!"

Tom shook his head. "In my opinion, that would be signing our own death warrants. Why would Wayne take a chance and let us live, once he has squeezed out all the information he wants?"

The logic of Tom's words sank home with crushing force. Bud and Ed, gripped by despondency, fell silent. But Tom himself had no time for despair. His brain was working at top speed, seeking a way out of their dilemma.

Suddenly his eye lighted upon a tray of rubies which had evidently been stored in the lab for polishing and cutting.

"Hold it, fellows!" Tom said hopefully. "Maybe there's another way to hold off Wayne and his cronies till help arrives!"

Even as he spoke, Tom's message-bearing rocket streaked down through the sky toward the base camp. Crewmen shouted in alarm as the whining missile caught their attention. But it sailed to earth in a neat glide—the homing device having guided its flight perfectly.

"B-b-brand my galley smokestack, what is it?" Chow bellowed as he ran to the spot.

"A dud, maybe," one crewman guessed.

"Not if it was fired here by the same rats who planted those land mines," Slim Davis retorted. "More likely it's booby-trapped!"

Arv, who had been one of the first to reach the rocket, scratched his jaw thoughtfully. "I'll bet you're all wrong," he muttered. "Ten to one it's from the skipper's space friends!"

His words drew an awed murmur of agreement. Months before, a missile from outer space had landed on the grounds of Swift Enterprises. It bore strange-looking symbols in a code which Tom and his father finally managed to translate. Later they had made radio contact with the senders and learned they were beings on another planet. Time and again since then they had come to the Swifts' aid when Tom or his father was in danger. Several times they had sent rockets.

"Wal, I'll be a horned toad!" Chow gasped. "Arv, you're right. Them space critters know Tom's in trouble and want to help. Why don't we open the thing and see what's inside?"

"And what if it's booby-trapped like Slim said?" another crewman objected. "It could blow the whole camp to smithereens!"

Arv himself was somewhat uneasy. More than once, the space beings had sent priceless specimens enclosed in rockets. These had had to be removed and handled with the utmost caution for scientific study. What if he and the others opened this rocket too hastily and spoiled some unique experiment?

"Before we touch it, I think we should radio Tom's dad for instructions," Arv argued.

The crewmen talked this over and agreed with Arv that it was the safest course. But when Dilling radioed Shopton, he received frustrating news.

"Mr. Swift's been called away on a secret mission connected with the rocket program," the Enterprises operator reported. "He may be back tomorrow, but he's incommunicado until then."

Dilling signed off without telling why he had called. The news would only alarm Mrs. Swift and Sandy. Arv called a council of war after hearing of Mr. Swift's absence.

"I vote we wait till noon tomorrow," Arv said. "Hank may have located the crash by that time. If not, we'll clear the camp and I'll open the rocket personally."

In spite of Chow's worried argument over the delay, the other crewmen agreed to wait.

During the night, Tom worked furiously in the underground laboratory of the mine. Bud and Ed watched as he constructed a device similar to the zircon-arc powered maser Bud had seen at Enterprises.

"At least I have a chance to use real rubies," Tom remarked wryly, as he ground out a slender rod from the biggest of the uncut stones. "Let's hope I can get a strong, clear signal to contact the outpost for help."

When the device was finished, Tom noted that the eight-o'clock deadline was uncomfortably close. Quickly he wrote out several pages of cleverly falsified data and formulas, then made some sketches.

The burning needlelike beam struck Gursk's wrist

But as he was about to signal with the maser, the prisoners heard the door being unbolted. "The rats!" Bud muttered. "They're five minutes early."

Wayne walked in, followed by Gursk, who was cradling a carbine. "Well?" Wayne demanded curtly.

Silently Tom handed him the papers. Wayne studied them with narrowed eyes. Then he looked up, smoldering with rage.

"Junk!" He crumpled the sheets viciously. "Did you think I'd fall for this eyewash? All right, Swift, you've tried to trick me again, so take the consequences!"

Gursk raised his carbine, aiming it at Ed Longstreet. Tom knew he had no choice but to use his ruby maser as a weapon. He snatched up the device and thumbed the switch.

A burning needlelike beam shot toward Gursk's hand!

Gursk dropped the carbine with a howl of agony and clutched his wrist, burned by the maser's intense heat. Bud dived for the weapon and seized it! Wayne lost no time. He hurled Gursk out the door and sprang after him, slamming and bolting the door behind him.

Moments later a roar of water was heard from the tunnel. Then Wayne's voice barked over a loud-speaker:

"Swift! Surrender or drown like rats in a trap!"

CHAPTER XX

JET RESCUE

WATER was already sluicing in under the door. Tom, Bud, and Ed eyed it with white faces, their hearts pounding like triphammers at the hideous danger facing them.

"What do we do now, skipper?" Bud endeavored to keep his voice steady. "Can't you try signaling the outpost with the ruby maser?"

But as Bud spoke, the fluorescent lights flickered out. The laboratory was plunged into darkness, except for the faint glow of daylight filtering down through the air shaft.

"There's your answer," Tom said grimly. "They must have switched off power from the generators—which means the maser's useless."

Already the trapped threesome were ankle-deep in the swirling, rising water.

Wayne's harsh voice came over the loud-speaker. *"How about it? Are you ready to surrender?"*

"Come on in and find out!" Bud roared back. "We're just waiting to grab that handlebar mustache of yours and shove your head under the water!"

Tom grinned at Bud's spirit.

Wayne replied with a snarl. *"All right! You punks are asking for it!"*

Tom sized up the situation rapidly. "We'll have to float up through the air shaft! It's wide enough for all three of us!"

As Ed started to move across the laboratory so he could peer up the shaft, Tom grabbed his arm. "Hold it! Remember there are guards at the top! They're probably all primed, waiting for us!"

Tom's words evidently carried, for a jeering laugh came rumbling and echoing down the shaft. "We're waiting, all right! It'll be like shooting fish in a barrel!"

"I'll fix it so we can get out!" Bud whispered to his companions. He edged along the wall, in order to approach the shaft opening under partial screening from a rack of tools. Holding the carbine belonging to Gursk out in front of him, he fired it up the shaft. The shot brought an oath of alarm from topside.

"Good work, pal," Tom murmured. "You've cleared the way!"

The water was rising faster and faster. Soon it was up to the boys' waists. Bud guarded the shaft opening, while Tom and Ed shoved a workbench underneath it for them to stand on.

In twenty minutes the laboratory was flooded. The three prisoners tread water to keep themselves chest-deep as they began floating upward. They pressed against one another, as well as the walls, for support. Tom and Ed supported Bud, so that he could hold the carbine high out of water.

"Some elevator!" Bud muttered wryly. The fifteen-foot shaft was filling rapidly.

"What happens when we spill over?" Ed asked with a tight grin.

"Run!" Tom advised. "If Bud can scare them back with a couple of quick shots, we might just reach cover."

None of the three really believed his words. The odds seemed hopeless. But all were determined to make a valiant effort.

"One thing in our favor," Tom reminded his companions, "is that they'll have to be grouped on one side of the shaft opening, or they'll be gunning one another—so we'll have a clear track!"

In moments now their heads would be poking above ground—targets for an enemy fusillade.

"Hey! What's that?" Bud cried.

The approaching hum of several jet aircraft could be heard. The boys heard yells of alarm outside the shaft. Then a silver-winged sky giant roared overhead.

"The *Sky Queen!*" Tom exulted. "And two cargo jets!"

Wayne and his men had gathered near the shaft opening, ready for the kill. But now they dashed in terror for the nearest tunnel entrance.

The planes gave them no chance to escape, wheeling and zooming in low, raking the ground with fiery blasts from their jet lifters! The *Sky Queen* hovered down and poised yards from the ground as Harlan Ames's voice roared over a power megaphone:

"Stay where you are! Throw your guns aside and get your hands up!"

Twenty minutes later the Swift crewmen had landed and the prisoners were bound. Tom, Bud, and Ed, still astonished at the rescue, were being given bear hugs and slaps on the back.

"Then you got our message from the rocket?" Tom asked.

"We were going to wait until noon," Arv replied sheepishly. "But just before dawn Chow got so curious he slipped out and opened the rocket on his own hook."

"Good old Chow!" Tom, Bud, and Ed exclaimed, and swamped the Texan with words of gratitude.

" 'Course I'm just a no-account ole cowboy who wouldn't savvy a mollycule or an electron if it bit me," Chow said with a proud grin. "But sometimes I ain't so all-fired slow on the uptake! Anyhow, these no-good sidewinders'll be put in gopher holes fer a long spell—that's what counts."

A few months later the Provard technical aid project in Kabulistan was moving forward in high gear. New villages, with electric power provided by Tom Swift's midget atomic power plants, were springing up in green farmlands watered by newly built irrigation canals. Schools, hospitals, factories, and mineral refining plants were on the drawing boards or already being built.

The ruby mine had proven so rich that it had given the Kabulistan government immediate financial stability. Numerous ore deposits had been located through the Swift aerial prospecting trips and would later add to the country's wealth. Tom subcontracted a number of technical projects to Flambo's Pan-Islamic Engineering Associates.

The young inventor felt that his own part in the vast undertaking was now completed, and that at last he could fly home to Shopton. He had plans for further inventions. His next one, the *Megascope Space Prober,* was to bring him further fame.

Before leaving Kabulistan, Tom and his friends were summoned to a special audience at the Shah's palace in Shirabad. The ruler himself made a presentation.

"In recognition of your great work in giving my country new strength and freedom," the Shah announced to a crowd of newsmen and diplomats, "I now bestow on you, Tom Swift Jr., Kabulistan's highest award—the Order of the Ruby!"

He proceeded to pin a jeweled medal on the chest of the embarrassed, yet pleased, young scientist. Other awards followed for Tom's companions.

In honor of Chow Winkler's special part in the rescue of Tom, Bud, and Ed, Habib Shah presented the beaming roly-poly cook with an ornate turban and a shimmering robe of rainbow-hued silk. As Tom shook hands with Chow, flash bulbs popped and television cameras recorded the scene.

"You can't top that getup, old-timer!" Tom whispered with a chuckle. "Better trade in your ten-gallon hat and all those wild sport shirts!"

Chow laughed gleefully. "Mebbe you're right, pardner. Just watch me make 'em popeyed in San Antone, wearin' these duds!"

Editor

Sara Connolly

Managing Editor

Ina Massler Levin, M.A.

Cover Artist

Denise Bauer

Art Production Manager

Kevin Barnes

Imaging

James Edward Grace

Publisher

Mary D. Smith, M.S. Ed.

Grades 2-3

Readers' Theater

Multicultural Stories

Ideal for Fluency Practice

Author

Diane Head

D1709203

Teacher Created Resources, Inc.

6421 Industry Way

Westminster, CA 92683

www.teachercreated.com

ISBN-1-4206-3067-9

©2006 Teacher Created Resources, Inc.

Made in U.S.A.

Table of Contents

Introduction

Readers' theater is a wonderful way to increase your students' fluency—and to build confidence, comprehension, and self-esteem. It's also a sure way to draw parents into your room and leave with a smile!

Readers' Theater: Multicultural Stories includes ten stories from around the world that have been adapted for young readers. Emergent and early fluent readers will love the repetitive nature of the scripts. The parts are written for small groups of children just beginning their literacy journey—with a proficient reader as narrator. These plays can be performed as true readers' theater using simple props, masks, or placards to identify characters. Puppet shows or live theater can be staged with the children inventing props and stage directions. The teacher's purpose and the children's skills in reading will guide your choice of play mode.

Included with each script is a story summary, a word list (excluding those words spoken by the narrator), the script, and several activities designed to build word skill, reading skills, and comprehension. Classroom teachers as well as teachers of specialized reading programs will enjoy using this collection. The word lists will help the teacher place children in appropriate plays.

Have fun reading and performing these plays! And enjoy the applause!

Sources consulted for the stories in this book:
Folk Tales and Fables of the World. Hayes, Barbara and Ingpen, Robert. Barnes and Noble, Inc., 1995.

The Young Oxford Book of Folk Tales. Crossley-Holland, Kevin (Editor). Oxford University Press, 1998.

How Maui Slowed the Sun

A Story from Hawaii

Multicultural Story Summary

All the people in Hawaii were sad because the days were too short for them to do all the things they wanted. The fisherman didn't have time to fish, the farmer couldn't get his crops in, Mother couldn't get her work done, and Maui didn't have time to play. So Maui came up with a plan. The days could be long enough for all. He captured the Sun with a rope and made the Sun promise to stay in the sky long enough for all of the people to do what they had to do. When the Sun promised, Maui let him go. That is how the Hawaiians explain their long summer days.

Setting

Hawaiian Island, with mountains and the seashore

Suggested Props

kite, fish in a basket, rake or hoe, rope

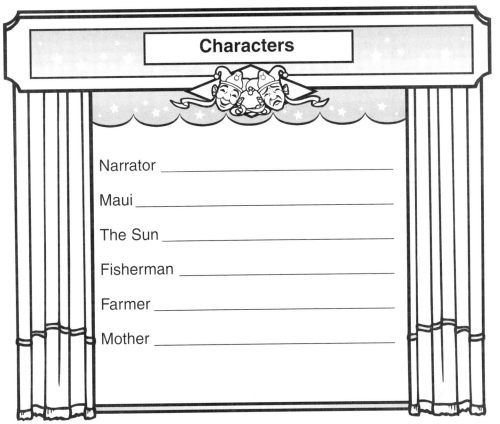

Characters

Narrator _____

Maui _____

The Sun _____

Fisherman _____

Farmer _____

Mother _____

How Maui Slowed the Sun

Word List

a	fly	more	sun
across	for	mother	that
all	from	move	the
am	fun	much	then
and	get	must	there
any	go	my	they
anyway	going	need	thing
are	good	needs	think
as	had	never	thinking
at	happy	no	this
away	have	not	time
bad	here	now	tired
be	his	oh	to
began	home	okay	too
but	how	on	up
can	I	one	wait
come	in	place	way
day	is	plants	well
deal	it	play	went
do	keep	please	what
does	kite	promise	who
doing	know	rope	why
down	let	say	will
either	let's	see	winter
every	like	short	with
farmer	look	sky	work
fast	make	so	yes
fish	many	some	you
fished	Maui	stop	your
fisherman	me	summer	

How Maui Slowed the Sun

Narrator:	Once upon a time, there was a boy named Maui. Maui and his mother lived on a beautiful Hawaiian island. Early one morning, in their little island house, Maui yawned and stretched.
Mother:	Maui! Get up!
Maui:	Okay, Mother.
Mother:	It is a good day!
Maui:	It is?
Mother:	Yes. Go play.
Narrator:	Maui looked of the window of their little hut. He saw that the weather was indeed perfect.
Mother:	What will you do?
Maui:	I will fly my kite!
Mother:	Good for you!
Narrator:	So out he went. He was happy to see how high the kite would soar up into the blue, blue sky.
Maui:	This is fun!
Mother:	You can fly the kite well!
Narrator:	Suddenly, he noticed the sun was setting. He could barely see his kite.
Mother:	Maui! Time to come in!
Maui:	Oh no! It can not be time to go home!
Mother:	Well, it is. Come on.
Narrator:	Maui wondered why the days seemed so short when he had so many fun things to do.
Maui:	Why does the sun go away so fast?
Mother:	I do not know, Maui.
Narrator:	Maui had asked a good question. But it was a question to which no one had an answer. The next day, Maui took his kite and walked along the beach. On his way, he met a fisherman.
Maui:	You do not look happy.

How Maui Slowed the Sun *(cont.)*

Fisherman:	No. I am not happy.
Maui:	Do you have any fish?
Fisherman:	No. Not one.
Maui:	No fish at all?
Fisherman:	No.
Maui:	That is bad.
Fisherman:	And I had a good place to fish, too.
Maui:	Yes?
Fisherman:	I fished, but then . . .
Maui:	What?
Fisherman:	The sun went down.
Maui:	Oh.
Fisherman:	So I have no fish.
Maui:	That is very bad.
Narrator:	Again, Maui had to wonder why the day was so very short.
Maui:	Why does the sun go away so fast?
Fisherman:	I do not know.
Narrator:	Maui kept on walking. He came to a sweet potato field.
Maui:	There is not much here.
Narrator:	Next, he came to a taro patch, expecting to see many plants.
Maui:	There is not much here, either.
Narrator:	Finally, he saw the farmer who owned both fields.
Maui:	You do not look happy.
Farmer:	No, I am not happy.
Maui:	Do you have any plants?

How Maui Slowed the Sun *(cont.)*

Farmer:	No. Not very many.
Maui:	No?
Farmer:	No.
Maui:	That is bad.
Farmer:	Yes, it is. I have a good place, too.
Maui:	Yes?
Farmer:	I began to work on my plants.
Maui:	And then what?
Farmer:	The sun went down. My plants do not get the sun they need.
Maui:	Oh.
Farmer:	And I have no time to work.
Maui:	That is very bad.
Narrator:	Again, Maui thought about why the day was so short.
Maui:	Why does the sun go away so fast?
Farmer:	I do not know.
Narrator:	Maui was puzzled. He decided to walk home and think a little on this. When he got home, he saw his mother sitting outside the hut, crying.
Maui:	What is it, Mother?
Mother:	I can not do all the work.
Maui:	That is bad.
Mother:	The day is too short.
Maui:	I think so, too.
Mother:	Why does the sun go away so fast?
Maui:	I have been thinking that, too, Mother.
Narrator:	Right then and there, Maui made an important decision.

8

How Maui Slowed the Sun *(cont.)*

Maui:	I will stop the sun from going so fast!
Mother:	How will you do that?
Narrator:	His mother stopped crying. Maui got busy coming up with a plan. He spent a lot of time watching the sun travel across the Hawaiian island. He observed it passing very close to the top of the island's volcano.
Maui:	I know what I will do! Mother?
Mother:	Yes, Maui?
Maui:	Can I have some rope?
Mother:	Yes, you can.
Narrator:	Maui sat right down and tied the strong ropes into lassoes. And then one dark night, he climbed to the top of the volcano.
Maui:	I will wait for the sun to come up.
Narrator:	And that is exactly what he did. Soon the sun came up. It barely cleared the rim of the volcano where Maui was hiding.
Maui:	Yes! There is the sun!
Narrator:	Maui jumped out from his hiding place. He tightly lassoed one of the sun's rays.
Sun:	What is going on here?
Maui:	There! I have you now!
Sun:	What?
Narrator:	The sun pulled and pulled as hard as he could. But Maui was stronger and he would not let go.
Sun:	Let me go!
Maui:	No way!
Sun:	Who are you, anyway?
Maui:	I am Maui.

How Maui Slowed the Sun *(cont.)*

Sun:	Why are you doing this? Let me go!
Maui:	Never!
Sun:	But why do you want me?
Maui:	The fisherman needs more time to fish.
Sun:	So?
Maui:	The farmer needs more time for his plants.
Sun:	So?
Maui:	Mother needs more time to do all the work.
Sun:	So?
Maui:	And I need more time to play!
Sun:	Oh! I see now! Well, let me go anyway.
Maui:	No. You must not go across the sky so fast.
Sun:	What? No way!
Maui:	Too bad, then. I have you.
Narrator:	Maui quickly picked up another strong rope. He lassoed another one of the sun's long rays.
Sun:	Now what is going on?
Maui:	I have you, Sun!
Sun:	Let me go!
Narrator:	The sun pulled and pulled. But Maui was still stronger than the sun. Pretty soon, Maui had lassoed too many of the sun's rays for it to get away. The sun was stuck in the sky!
Sun:	Let me go!
Maui:	Say you will not go so fast!
Sun:	No way!
Maui:	Too bad for you, then.

How Maui Slowed the Sun *(cont.)*

Narrator:	The battle went on for a very long time. Finally, the sun was exhausted.
Sun:	Stop, Maui!
Maui:	I will not let you go, Sun.
Sun:	Let's make a deal.
Maui:	What is the deal?
Sun:	I will go not so fast in the summer.
Maui:	And in the winter?
Sun:	I will move as I like.
Maui:	Will you keep your promise?
Sun:	Yes, I will.
Maui:	How can I know that?
Sun:	I am tired, Maui.
Maui:	Well . . .
Sun:	Please let me go. I promise.
Maui:	Okay.
Narrator:	And so it was that a deal was made between Maui and the sun. The sun kept his promise to move more slowly across the sky in the summer. In the winter, the sun could move more quickly. Maui ran to tell his friends.
Maui:	Well, how do you like that?
Fisherman:	I have more time to fish now!
Farmer:	I have more time with my plants now!
Mother:	I have more time to do all the work now!
Maui:	And I have more time to play now!
Narrator:	And that is why the days are longer in the summer—because Maui found a way to slow the sun.

The End

How Maui Slowed the Sun *(cont.)*

Mini-Lessons and Activities

- **Explore other Hawaiian folk tales. Possible resources:**

  1. *Hawaiian Myths of Earth, Sea, and Sky* by Vivian L. Thompson. Kolowalu Book, University of Hawaii Press, 1966.
  2. *The Young Oxford Book of Folk Tales* by Kevin Crossley-Holland. Oxford University Press, Oxford, 1988.
  3. *Hawaiian Legends of Tricksters and Riddlers* by Vivian L. Thompson. Kolowalu Book, University of Hawaii Press, 1969.

- **Comparison Chart**

  Students can use this chart to make comparisons between "Maui" and shared stories from authentic Hawaiian literature. It could also be used to compare a Hawaiian tale with a tale from another culture.

Comparison Chart	Title/Author	Title/Author
Setting		
Characters		
Problem		
Resolution		
Timeline		

- **Mini-lesson on Voice Intonation**

  Emergent readers need to know how to read when they encounter different punctuation marks. First, they need to recognize the punctuation marks, such as /. , ! ?/. Have them circle the punctuation marks on the first page of the text. Explain that the reader's voice should "go down" at the mark of the period. The reader should pause just for a second at the comma. The voice should "go up" for a question mark and should express surprise, dismay, or pleasure at the exclamation point.   This is called "reading the punctuation." The teacher should model the correct voice intonation and have the children practice with him or her. Students could also draw a happy face, angry face, or surprised face to show the proper emotion to use on different lines of text.

- **Mini-lesson on Using /ing/**

  The word list contains the following /ing/ words: going, doing, thinking

  These words can be taken from the word list to give the children practice in adding the /ing/ ending: work, will, want, wait, see, play, plant, need, be, fish, keep, know, look.

Baba Yaga and the Girl

A Story from Russia

Multicultural Story Summary

An evil stepmother sends her stepdaughter to a witch's house hoping to be rid of her once and for all. The girl first walks to her auntie's house, where she learns that she is in great danger from Baba Yaga. The auntie gives her advice on how to escape the witch. The girl goes to the witch's house. She is kind to Baba Yaga's maid and gives her a scarf. She gives the cat some meat, the dog some bread, the tree a ribbon, and the gate some oil. Because of her kindness, they let her pass. When Baba Yaga finds the girl gone, she goes after her. Baba Yaga is angry that the girl has gotten by her creatures. As she nears the girl, the girl throws out a magic towel to create a river. This doesn't stop angry Baba Yaga. Then the girl throws out a magic comb which becomes a forest that Baba Yaga cannot penetrate. The girl returns home safely and the stepmother's unkindness is discovered.

Setting

The witch's house in a dark forest.

Suggested Props

ribbon, basket, oil can, bread, meat, scarf, towel, comb

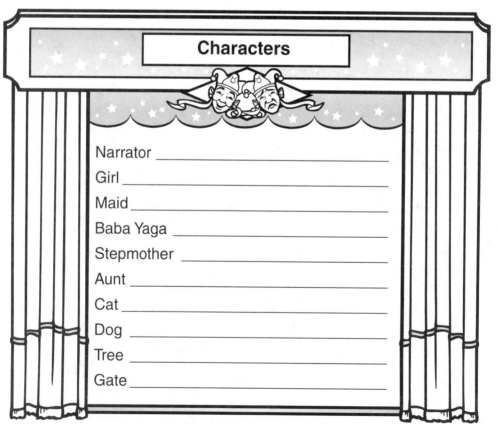

Characters

Narrator _____

Girl _____

Maid _____

Baba Yaga _____

Stepmother _____

Aunt _____

Cat _____

Dog _____

Tree _____

Gate _____

Baba Yaga and the Girl *(cont.)*

Word List

a	do	hot	one	too
after	dog	house	out	towel
all	don't	I	please	tree
am	down	if	present	trees
and	eat	in	put	tree's
are	ever	is	ribbon	tricking
as	feed	it	right	up
at	fire	just	river	use
auntie	footsteps	know	run	very
away	for	let	saved	wait
Baba Yaga	forest	listen	scarf	want
Baba Yaga's	from	look	scratch	wants
bad	gate	mad	see	wash
basket	gave	maid	she	water
be	get	make	sister's	way
before	girl	maybe	slow	welcome
bite	glad	me	so	well
branches	go	meat	some	what
bread	going	mother	stop	when
but	good	must	take	where
by	ha	my	tell	who
can	has	need	thank	why
cat	have	needle	that	will
catch	heat	never	the	works
close	hello	no	them	yes
comb	helped	not	there	you
come	her	of	this	you're
coming	here	oh	thread	
cross	hit	oil	tie	
dear	home	okay	time	
did	hope	on	to	

Baba Yaga and the Girl

Narrator:	Once upon a time in a far away land called Russia, there lived a little girl. She lived in a little cottage near a deep, dark forest. Her father was a very busy man and his new wife, the girl's stepmother, didn't particularly like little girls. One day, the stepmother told the girl to run an errand for her. However, what the evil woman really wanted was to be rid of the girl once and for all.
Stepmother:	Girl, you will go to my sister's house.
Girl:	Okay. I will do that.
Stepmother:	Get a needle and thread. I will make a shirt.
Girl:	Okay.
Stepmother:	I will know if you do not do as I tell you.
Girl:	Here I go.
Narrator:	Now the stepmother pretended to give the girl directions to her sister's house, but it was all a lie. She really gave directions to Baba Yaga's house. Baba Yaga was an evil witch who lived in the forest. Lucky for the little girl, she distrusted her stepmother. After fetching her basket, she put on a pretty scarf and went first to her own auntie's house.
Aunt:	Hello, dear!
Girl:	Hello, auntie.
Aunt:	I am glad to see you!
Girl:	Thank you. I am glad to see you, too!
Aunt:	But why are you here?
Narrator:	The girl told her aunt what the stepmother had said. . . directions included.
Aunt:	That is not right at all!
Girl:	What?
Aunt:	You will be at Baba Yaga's house!

Baba Yaga and the Girl *(cont.)*

Girl:	Who is Baba Yaga?
Aunt:	She is very, very bad!
Girl:	Oh, no!
Aunt:	Baba Yaga will eat you up!
Girl:	Oh, no!
Aunt:	Baba Yaga has a tree that will hit you.
Girl:	Oh, what can I do?
Aunt:	Take this ribbon.
Girl:	Okay.
Aunt:	Tie up the tree's branches.
Girl:	Okay. I will do that.
Aunt:	Baba Yaga has a gate that will catch you.
Girl:	Oh, what can I do?
Aunt:	Take this oil.
Girl:	Okay.
Aunt:	Oil the gate.
Girl:	Okay. I will do that.
Aunt:	She has a dog that will bite you.
Girl:	Oh, what can I do?
Aunt:	Take this bread.
Girl:	Okay.
Aunt:	Feed the dog.
Girl:	Okay. I will do that.
Aunt:	Baba Yaga has a cat that will scratch you.
Girl:	Oh, what can I do?
Aunt:	Take this meat.
Girl:	Okay.
Aunt:	Feed the cat.
Girl:	Okay. I will do that. Thank you, Auntie.

Baba Yaga and the Girl *(cont.)*

Narrator:	The girl took all the things her good auntie had given her, put them in her basket, and went on her way. She was terrified of meeting Baba Yaga. But in many ways, she was even more scared of disobeying her stepmother and being found out. Soon she came to Baba Yaga's cottage. The old witch was sitting on the porch.
Girl:	Hello.
Baba Yaga:	What do you want?
Girl:	My mother wants a needle and thread.
Baba Yaga:	Is that so?
Girl:	Yes. Do you have them?
Baba Yaga:	Maybe. Come in. I will look.
Narrator:	The girl gulped, but she followed Baba Yaga inside. Baba Yaga's cottage was just as horrible as her auntie had said. There was no question that the stepmother was trying to do her harm now.
Baba Yaga:	Wait here.
Girl:	Okay.
Narrator:	Baba Yaga rubbed her evil hands together. Dinner had walked right into her cottage!
Baba Yaga:	Where is my maid?
Maid:	Here I am.
Baba Yaga:	A girl is here.
Maid:	I see.
Baba Yaga:	Make a fire.
Maid:	Okay. I will do that.
Baba Yaga:	Heat some water so she can wash.
Maid:	Yes, I will do that.
Baba Yaga:	She will be good to eat.

Baba Yaga and the Girl *(cont.)*

Narrator:	The little girl overheard Baba Yaga. She was panic-stricken! And then she thought of what her auntie had told her. She came up with a plan while Baba Yaga was outside gathering herbs to put in the cooking pot.
Girl:	Maid! The fire is too hot!
Maid:	It is?
Girl:	Yes. You need to put water on it.
Maid:	I do?
Girl:	Yes, you do. Here. Use my basket for the water.
Maid:	Thank you. No one ever helped me before.
Girl:	You're welcome.
Narrator:	The maid put just enough water on the fire so it didn't go out completely. Still, it wasn't hot enough to cook anything properly.
Girl:	Thank you! You have saved me! Please take my scarf!
Maid:	No one ever gave me a present before. Thank you.
Narrator:	And so the maid became the girl's friend. Just then, an angry cat came into the cottage. It was hissing and scratching.
Girl:	Here, cat.
Cat:	What?
Girl:	Have some meat.
Cat:	Thank you. No one ever gave me meat before.
Girl:	You're welcome. Can you tell me how to get out of here?
Cat:	Yes, I can. Take this towel and this comb.
Girl:	Okay.
Cat:	Then run away. Go that way.
Girl:	But Baba Yaga will come after me.
Cat:	Yes, she will.

Baba Yaga and the Girl *(cont.)*

Girl:	Oh, no!
Cat:	Listen for her footsteps.
Girl:	Okay.
Cat:	When she is close, put down the towel.
Girl:	Why?
Cat:	It will make a river.
Girl:	A river?
Cat:	Yes. It will take time for Baba Yaga to cross the river.
Girl:	That is good.
Cat:	Baba Yaga will come after you.
Girl:	And she will be mad!
Cat:	Yes, she will. Listen for her footsteps.
Girl:	Okay.
Cat:	When she is close, put down the comb.
Girl:	Why?
Cat:	It will make trees.
Girl:	Trees?
Cat:	The trees will slow her down.
Girl:	That is good.
Cat:	Maybe she will stop coming after you and go home.
Girl:	Thank you, cat.
Narrator:	The girl took the towel and comb. She put them into her basket and ran from the witch's house. The dog in the yard watched her. He growled at her. Then he ran after her, his teeth bared.
Girl:	Here, dog.
Dog:	What?
Girl:	Have some bread.

Baba Yaga and the Girl (*cont.*)

Dog:	Thank you. No one ever gave me bread before.
Girl:	You're welcome. Can you let me get out of here?
Dog:	Yes. I can do that.
Narrator:	The girl went safely by and came to the gate. It slammed shut in her face.
Girl:	Here, gate.
Gate:	What?
Girl:	Have some oil.
Gate:	Thank you. No one ever gave me oil before.
Girl:	You're welcome. Can you let me get out of here?
Gate:	Yes. I can do that.
Narrator:	The girl passed through the quiet gate. Then she came to the tree. It whipped its branches at her.
Girl:	Here, tree.
Tree:	What?
Girl:	Have a ribbon.
Tree:	Thank you. No one ever gave me a ribbon before.
Girl:	You're welcome. Can you let me get out of here?
Tree:	Yes. I can do that.
Narrator:	Just then Baba Yaga came back with her fresh soup herbs.
Baba Yaga:	Where are you, girl?
Narrator:	At that very moment, the cat decided to give the girl some more help.
Cat:	Baba Yaga!
Baba Yaga:	Yes?
Cat:	Here I am!
Baba Yaga:	Good!

Baba Yaga and the Girl *(cont.)*

Narrator:	Baba Yaga went to see. She was surprised to find the cat, just finishing off his last bit of meat. She became angry.
Baba Yaga:	You are not the girl!
Cat:	No. I am just a cat.
Baba Yaga:	Why are you tricking me, cat?
Cat:	You never gave me meat.
Baba Yaga:	So what?
Cat:	The girl gave me meat. So there.
Narrator:	That made Baba Yaga even angrier. She stamped out of the house to see the dog.
Baba Yaga:	Dog! Where is the girl?
Dog:	I don't know.
Baba Yaga:	She must have come by you.
Dog:	Well, yes, I did see her.
Baba Yaga:	Where is she?
Dog:	I don't know.
Baba Yaga:	Why didn't you stop her?
Dog:	You never gave me bread.
Baba Yaga:	So what?
Dog:	The girl gave me bread. So there.
Narrator:	Baba Yaga was furious. She stormed up to the gate.
Baba Yaga:	Gate! Where is the girl?
Gate:	I don't know.
Baba Yaga:	She must have come by you.
Gate:	Well, yes, I did see her.
Baba Yaga:	Why didn't you stop her?

Baba Yaga and the Girl *(cont.)*

Gate:	You never gave me oil.
Baba Yaga:	So what?
Gate:	The girl gave me oil. So there.
Narrator:	Baba Yaga had steam coming from her ears—that's how mad she was! She stomped up to the tree.
Baba Yaga:	Tree! Where is the girl?
Tree:	I don't know.
Baba Yaga:	She must have come by you.
Tree:	Well, yes, I did see her.
Baba Yaga:	And where did you get that ribbon?
Tree:	It is from the girl.
Baba Yaga:	And so you let her go?
Tree:	Yes, I did.
Baba Yaga:	Why didn't you stop her?
Tree:	You never gave me a ribbon.
Baba Yaga:	I know! And the girl did!
Tree:	Yes, she did. So there.
Narrator:	Just then, the maid leaned out of the window of **Baba Yaga's** hut. She waved her new scarf at Baba Yaga.
Maid:	See this scarf?
Baba Yaga:	Yes, I do.
Maid:	The girl gave it to me.
Baba Yaga:	And?
Maid:	And so I helped her, too!
Narrator:	Baba Yaga screamed with rage! She hobbled **down the road,** determined to catch the girl and boil her for dinner. **Far down** the road, the girl heard Baba Yaga's muttering and **stomping.**
Girl:	What is that?
Baba Yaga:	Girl! Girl!

Baba Yaga and the Girl *(cont.)*

Girl:	Oh, no! Baba Yaga is coming!
Narrator:	Then she remembered what the cat had told her to do when Baba Yaga got too close.
Girl:	Where is that towel?
Narrator:	She took the towel from her basket and tossed it down. Suddenly, a river appeared between the girl and the witch.
Girl:	I hope that works!
Narrator:	Baba Yaga came to the river.
Baba Yaga:	A river! Ha!
Narrator:	She waded right in. Too bad she was so angry, though—the water turned to steam and evaporated. She kept tromping after the girl.
Girl:	What is that? Oh, no! Baba Yaga is coming!
Narrator:	Again, she remembered what the cat had told her to do.
Girl:	Where is that comb?
Narrator:	She rummaged through her basket and threw down the magic comb. A thick forest sprang up between the girl and the furious witch.
Girl:	I hope that works!
Narrator:	Baba Yaga came to the forest.
Baba Yaga:	What!? A forest?
Narrator:	She worked a long time trying to squeeze through all the trees, but it was no use.
Baba Yaga:	I am going home!
Narrator:	The girl arrived home safely and told her father all that had happened. The evil stepmother went away and never came back. Baba Yaga returned to her hut and went hungry. And although she eventually forgot about the girl, she didn't stop causing trouble.

The End

Baba Yaga and the Girl *(cont.)*

Mini-Lessons and Activities

- **Read in Character**

Show the children what fun it is to use a new voice when acting in a play or simply reading a story. Modeling is the best way to do this - whether it is during a read-aloud time or from listening to a book on tape. Explain to the children that when you read the part of an evil character, you try to make your voice sound mean and scary. Read a few lines of Baba Yaga's part, making your voice sound mean. Have the children echo your reading. A good character, like the girl in Baba Yaga, could sound very happy and friendly. Again, model what a good character's voice might sound like. Encourage the children to add a purr for the cat's voice or a growl in the dog's voice. Demonstrate for the children that when the character is surprised or unhappy, the good reader's voice echoes that emotion.

- **Elements of the Fairy Tale**

After reading several fairy tales, form small groups of children to discover and discuss the following elements of the fairy tale: beginnings, settings, events happening in 3's, elements of magic, talking animals, evil vs. good. Children can record their discoveries on large pieces of paper to make a chart. As they learn more about the fairy tale, they can add to their chart.

- **Story Sequence**

Construct a simple story map using the children's drawings in order to show the sequence of important events in Baba Yaga. Include: the girl's house, the path through the forest to the aunt's house, the path to Baba Yaga's hut, the location of the gate, the dog and the tree, the places where the girl drops her comb and towel to stop Baba Yaga. The children can take turns sharing their maps with a partner. The maps can also be used in story retelling.

- **Word Work—Spelling Patterns**

Be sure the children understand what consonants and vowels are. Explain that there are words with long vowels sounds and words with short vowel sounds. Many English words follow certain spelling patterns. Give pairs of children three large cards with the following spelling patterns printing on them: CVC pattern, CVVC pattern, and CVCe pattern. These cards will be used as the template for the words. Give the children small cards with the following words from the story: dog, cat, did, hit, let, yes, not, can, run, put, dear, wait, heat, maid, meat, need, feed, fire, gate, gave, here, home, hope, make, time. The children may work together to put the words under the proper spelling pattern card. For this particular activity, the CVC pattern will have 10 words, the CVVC pattern will have seven words, and the CVCe pattern will have eight words. As an extension, see if the children can come up with more words that follow each of these patterns.

The Leather Bag

A Story from Korea

Multicultural Story Summary

A boy's faithful servant tells him wonderful stories, which live inside a leather bag. They can only be freed when told to someone else, but the boy is selfish and won't tell the stories. The stories become too crowded in the bag and begin to fight. They plot to harm the boy, who by this time has grown into a man. The servant overhears their plan to do away with the man as he travels to his wedding. The fox plans to have the water story in the well drown the boy. The tiger plans to have his friend, the strawberry story, get him in the strawberry field. The bat plans to get him when he steps off his horse onto a bag of rice and falls. The snake plans to have another snake under the man's sleeping mat. The servant goes along with the man and foils all the evil plans. He convinces the boy to share the stories, thereby letting them out of the crowded bag.

Setting

The boy's house is at one end of the stage and a church is at the other. Between them is a long road.

Suggested Props

brown bag, sword

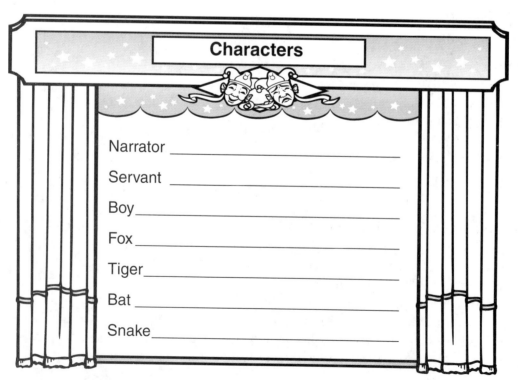

Characters

Narrator _____

Servant _____

Boy_____

Fox_____

Tiger_____

Bat _____

Snake_____

The Leather Bag *(cont.)*

Word List

a	free	know	please	thirsty
about	friend	leave	pushing	this
all	friends	let	put	tigers
and	get	let's	rice	time
are	gets	life	room	tip
ask	go	like	said	tired
at	goes	long	saved	to
bad	going	look	sleep	told
bag	good	mad	sleeping	too
be	great	make	smells	trip
been	have	married	snake	under
best	he	mat	so	us
boy	here	me	some	want
can	heroes	might	sorry	water
clothes	hey	more	stop	we
come	hide	must	stops	well
did	him	my	stories	what
do	his	need	story	when
does	horse	new	strawberries	why
doesn't	hot	nice	strawberry	will
dragons	hungry	no	stuck	wish
drink	hurt	not	sure	with
eat	I	of	take	work
fair	idea	off	tell	would
fairies	if	oh	thank	yes
fall	in	okay	that	you
far	is	old	the	your
feet	isn't	on	then	
field	it	out	there	
food	keeping	over	they	
for	kept	place	think	

The Leather Bag

Narrator:	Once upon a time, in the faraway land of Korea, there lived a boy who loved listening to old fairy stories. Every evening, his servant sat at his bedside and told him a wonderful story.
Boy:	Tell me a story!
Servant:	Okay. Would you like a story about dragons?
Boy:	Yes! I like dragons!
Servant:	Or would you like a story about tigers?
Boy:	Yes! I like tigers!
Servant:	Do you like stories about good fairies?
Boy:	Yes!
Servant:	Do you like stories about great heroes?
Boy:	Oh, yes! I like hero stories the best!
Narrator:	As the servant told stories to the boy, the stories had to go into an old leather bag. It hung by a drawstring behind the boy's closet door. They had to remain there until the boy shared the stories with someone else.
Servant:	Will you tell the stories?
Boy:	No! They are my stories!
Servant:	But you must tell the stories!
Boy:	No! I will not!
Narrator:	You see, the boy was selfish with the wonderful stories. And as time passed and the boy grew, the stories inside the bag got smashed together.
Fox:	We want out!
Tiger:	Please tell my story!
Bat:	There is no room!
Snake:	Stop pushing!

The Leather Bag *(cont.)*

Narrator:	Time passed. The boy grew into a young man. Still, every evening, the servant would tell a story. The leather bag was too full now and yet the selfish young man wouldn't share. The stories grew angry. And then the evil stories hatched a terrible plan. The good stories were afraid of the evil stories and so they kept quiet.
Fox:	No more stories!
Tiger:	I said let us out!
Bat:	There is no more room!
Snake:	Hey! Stop pushing!
Narrator:	There came a time when the young man wanted a wife. The servant was asked to pack for the trip. When he went into the young man's bedroom to pack the trunks, he was surprised to hear little voices coming from behind the door.
Fox:	So he is to be married.
Tiger:	Yes. He will have good food and new clothes.
Bat:	And we are stuck in here.
Snake:	It is not fair.
Fox:	He will leave us in this old bag.
Tiger:	We have been here a long, long time.
Bat:	Too long.
Snake:	Let's get him. Then we can come out.
Fox:	There is a good idea!
Tiger:	It would be nice to be free.
Bat:	Yes, it would.
Snake:	Let's do it.
Narrator:	The servant peered into the leather bag. It bulged with untold stories. It wiggled and jiggled. Its sides pooched out as the angry stories argued. The servant listened as the stories continued making their evil plans.
Fox:	It is a long trip.

The Leather Bag *(cont.)*

Tiger:	Yes, it is.
Fox:	He will be hot and he will get thirsty.
Bat:	Yes, he will.
Fox:	The water story is one of my friends.
Snake:	He is?
Fox:	Yes. I will ask him to hide in the well.
Tiger:	And then what?
Fox:	When the boy stops for a drink, the water story will get him!
Bat:	That might work.
Snake:	Yes, it might. But what if it doesn't?
Narrator:	The old servant's eyes grew wide as he listened, but he didn't interrupt. He had to know the extent of the evil plan.
Tiger:	It is a long trip.
Fox:	Yes, it is.
Tiger:	He will be hungry.
Bat:	Yes, he will.
Tiger:	The strawberry story is one of my friends.
Snake:	He is?
Tiger:	Yes. I will ask my friend to hide in the strawberry field.
Fox:	Then what?
Tiger:	When he stops to eat, the strawberry story will get him!
Bat:	That might work.
Snake:	Yes, it might. But what if it doesn't?
Narrator:	The faithful servant kept listening because he loved the young man in spite of his selfish behavior with the wonderful stories. The bag wiggled some more.
Bat:	It is a long trip.
Fox:	Yes, it is.
Bat:	When he gets there, he will have to get off his horse.
Tiger:	Yes, he will.

The Leather Bag *(cont.)*

Bat:	I will make sure a bag of rice is put under his feet.
Snake:	And then what?
Bat:	When he gets off, he will fall off the bag of rice!
Fox:	That might work.
Tiger:	Yes, it might.
Snake:	But what if it doesn't?
Narrator:	The servant leaned closer to listen some more. Not only was he a wonderful storyteller, he was also an excellent listener.
Snake:	It is a long trip.
Fox:	Yes, it is.
Snake:	When he gets there he will have to sleep.
Tiger:	Yes, he will.
Snake:	I will make sure a snake is under his sleeping mat.
Bat:	And then what?
Snake:	When he goes to sleep, the snake will get him!
Fox:	That might work.
Tiger:	Yes, it might.
Snake:	Then he will be sorry for keeping us in this bag for so long.
Narrator:	The old servant felt awful. He wanted to tell the young man what he knew, but he was sure his master would not believe him. He tried to think of a way to save his master. Finally, he had the solution. He went to the young man.
Servant:	Please take me with you on your trip.
Boy:	No. It is too far and you are too old.
Servant:	Please? I would like to go with you.
Boy:	Okay. You can come, too.
Narrator:	So they packed their belongings and off they went. The old servant led the young man's horse. After riding for some time, the young man became thirsty. The servant remembered what he had heard.

The Leather Bag (cont.)

Boy: Let's stop. I need some water.

Servant: We cannot stop.

Boy: Why not?

Servant: The water smells bad.

Boy: It does?

Servant: Yes, it does.

Narrator: Of course, the water was fine, but the old servant knew what the fox story had said about the dangers near the well. The servant was glad to have saved his master's life. So they went on down the road. Soon they passed a field of strawberries.

Boy: Let's stop. I want a strawberry.

Servant: We cannot stop.

Boy: Why not?

Servant: The strawberries are not good.

Boy: But they look good.

Servant: No. They are not good at all.

Narrator: And so they went on their way and the old servant was happy because the young man's life had been spared once again.   In time, they arrived at their destination. The old servant saw a bag of rice in the yard, just as the stories had said.

Boy: Let me get off the horse.

Servant: No. We cannot stop here.

Boy: Why not?

Servant: That bag will tip over and you will fall.

Boy: It will?

Servant: Yes, it will.

Narrator: And that was how the young man was saved from a third time. The old servant was very happy.

Boy: I am tired.

Servant: You are?

The Leather Bag *(cont.)*

Boy: Yes. I will sleep here.

Servant: Here? This is not a good place to sleep.

Boy: It isn't?

Servant; No, not at all!

Narrator: Suddenly, the old servant drew his sword and slashed down on the mat the young man was to sleep upon. He killed the snake that lurked beneath the mat.

Boy: What is going on here?

Servant: The stories are mad. They wish to hurt you.

Boy: What stories?

Servant: There are stories in the bag.

Boy: I did not know that! You saved my life!

Servant: Yes, I think I did.

Boy: Thank you. But why are the stories mad?

Servant: Stories need to be told. They have no more room in the bag if they are not told.

Boy: And I have kept them in there.

Servant: Yes. You must tell the stories.

Boy: I will do that. Thank you!

Narrator: After that, the young man forgot his selfish ways and told a different story every evening, just as the servant had done for him. He turned out to be an excellent storyteller. The stories were released one by one and there was no more complaining in the leather bag because there was no more crowding. And the old servant was content to live out his days with the young man, his family, and the stories.

The End

The Leather Bag *(cont.)*

Mini-Lessons and Activities

- **Voice/Volume**

When giving a play, it is vital that the audience hears what the actors are saying, especially if you are performing readers' theater selections. In readers' theater there is very little action to help the audience understand the plot. Encourage the children to use their "playground voices" when reading and performing. It might be helpful to have the students pair up and take turns at projecting their voices to the back of the room. Have the partners decide if the words they heard their partner say were clear enough and loud enough to be understood at a distance. Remind the students of how sound carries. If their heads are down, their voices cannot be heard at a distance. If their heads are up, their voice is more likely to be heard at the back of the room.

- **Comprehension**

As an added attraction to the play, you might have the students create a visual interpretation of the story to use during the presentation. Have the children choose the important scenes of the story as a group. Then they can create visuals on poster board. The pictures should help the audience understand the story. Students who do not wish to draw can decorate the posters, write in a caption, or hold and flip the displays during the performance.

- **Learning About Settings**

In folk tales, some settings are global and some are more specific. Often, the props used in a play help us to understand the setting and time of the story. Have the children explore the places the characters "visit" in The Leather Bag. The following words and phrases may help the children understand more about the setting of this play: the boy's home has a servant, Korea, long ago, traveling to get a wife, riding horses, the well, strawberry fields, rice bags, sleeping mats, sword. You might use a chart or draw pictures to help the students get a better understanding of this particular story's setting.

- **The Powerful /r/ - Word**

/r/ is a very powerful letter! When /r/ is placed after a vowel, often we cannot "hear" the vowel at all. Make a chart with the following words from the story as headings: far, over, thirsty, for, hurt. Underline the vowel and the /r/. Have the children put the following story words in the appropriate column: horse, sure, more, story, work, under, water, tiger. See if they can come up with additional words to place under the /ir/ and /ar/ columns.

Momotaro, The Peach Boy

A Story from Japan

Multicultural Story Summary

A magical peach comes to an old couple. Inside the peach is a boy who becomes a great warrior. He wants to free Japan of the demons that live on an island. The demons have stolen the peoples' riches. Momotaro makes friends of the dog, the monkey, and the bird along the way to the demons' island. Although the animals do not get along at first, Momotaro teaches them to work together to invade the demons' castle and fight to get the stolen riches returned to the people.

Setting

On one end of the stage, there is a cottage. At the other end, there is the demons' island. Between them is a forest and the ocean.

Suggested Props

rice cakes, sword, jewelry box, stick

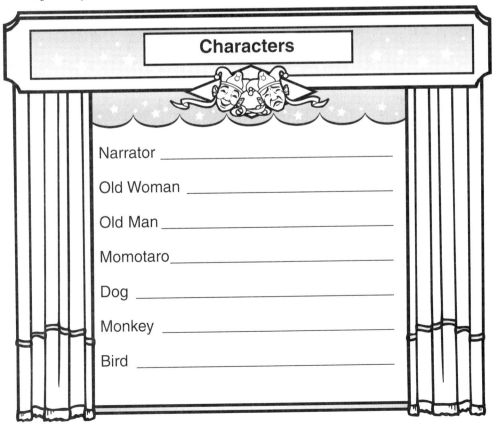

Characters

Narrator _____

Old Woman _____

Old Man _____

Momotaro_____

Dog _____

Monkey _____

Bird _____

Momotaro, The Peach Boy

Word List

a	demons	here	of	stop
about	did	he's	oh	stream
afraid	dinner	him	on	take
all	do	home	one	tell
am	dog	hungry	open	that
an	doing	hurray	opens	the
and	don't	I	or	them
are	down	in	over	then
at	eat	is	peach	there
away	either	island	peck	they
back	father	it	people	things
be	fighting	just	pull	this
beg	flips	know	quiet	to
big	fly	land	ready	today
bird	food	laughed	rice	too
bite	for	let	rid	took
boat	found	let's	roof	trip
but	from	long	rude	up
by	gate	look	safe	up
bye	get	make	said	us
cake	give	matter	say	very
cakes	glad	may	sea	walls
can	go	me	see	was
can't	going	Momotaro	send	wash
care	good	monkey	sing	way
climb	hair	mother	so	we
clothes	have	my	some	what
come	he	nice	son	when
cut	hear	no	sorry	who
day	heard	not	stay	why
demon	help	now	steal	will

Momotaro, The Peach Boy

Narrator:	Once upon a time, in far off Japan, there lived an old man and an old woman. They were very poor, but they were happy except for one thing—they had no children to comfort them in their old age.
Old Woman:	It is a nice day!
Old Man:	What will you do today?
Old Woman:	I will wash the clothes.
Old Man:	Take care down by the stream.
Old Woman:	I will.
Narrator:	So the old woman went off to wash clothes on that fine spring day. Suddenly something huge came floating down the stream.
Old Woman:	What is this? A peach!! It is big! It will make a good dinner for us!
Narrator:	She raked the peach in towards the bank of the river with a big stick.
Old Woman:	I am glad I found this peach!
Narrator:	She carried the peach home. At dinnertime, the old man came home from his work in the fields.
Old Woman:	Look! See what I found in the stream?
Old Man:	A peach! Good! I am very hungry. Let's eat it.
Old Woman:	Yes! It will be good.
Narrator:	They were just about to cut the peach in half when they heard a little voice.
Momotaro:	Stop! Do not cut the peach!
Old Man:	Did you hear that?
Old Woman:	Yes, I did.
Old Man:	What was that?
Old Woman:	I do not know!
Old Man:	Who said that?
Narrator:	In an instant, the peach split open and out jumped a little boy.

Momotaro, The Peach Boy *(cont.)*

Old Man and Old Woman:	Oh my!
Momotaro:	I am Momotaro. I will be your son.
Old Man and Old Woman:	We will be glad to have you.
Narrator:	And the old couple was delighted with the little boy. They were good parents to him. Momotaro quickly grew up brave and smart and strong. One day, Momotaro went to his parents.
Momotaro:	Father! Mother! I have to go away.
Old Man:	Why?
Momotaro:	There is an island of demons in the sea.
Old Man:	I have heard that.
Momotaro:	They steal from good people.
Old Man:	I have heard that, too.
Momotaro:	I will get rid of them and give what they took back to the people.
Old Woman:	Will you be back, son?
Momotaro:	Yes, I will.
Old Man:	Then I will get your things.
Old Woman:	And I will get you some rice cakes to eat on the way.
Narrator:	Soon they were back with Momotaro's things.
Old Woman:	Good bye, my son.
Old Man:	Good bye, son. Be safe.
Momotaro:	I will be back!
Narrator:	Momotaro went on down the road to the sea. Soon he became hungry. He sat down to eat a rice cake. To his surprise, a large dog jumped out from behind some bushes.
Dog:	Why are you here?
Momotaro:	I am on a trip.
Dog:	You are on my land.

Momotaro, The Peach Boy *(cont.)*

Momotaro:	Yes, I am. But not for long.
Dog:	Give me some food or I will bite you.
Momotaro:	Oh no, you won't.
Dog:	I won't?
Momotaro:	No. I am going to get rid of the demons.
Dog:	You are?
Momotaro:	Yes. I will give back the things they took from the people.
Dog:	I am sorry I was rude. Please let me go with you.
Momotaro:	Dog, you may go. Here is a rice cake.
Narrator:	They finished eating and went on their way. Deep in the jungle, they were surprised by a hairy monkey.
Monkey:	Why are you here?
Momotaro:	I am on a trip.
Monkey:	You are on my land.
Momotaro:	Yes, I am. But not for long.
Monkey:	Give me some food or I will pull your hair.
Momotaro:	Oh no, you won't.
Monkey:	I won't?
Momotaro:	No. I am going to get rid of the demons.
Monkey:	You are?
Momotaro:	Yes. I will give back the things they took from the people.
Monkey:	I am sorry I was rude. Please let me go with you.
Dog:	What? He can't go!
Momotaro:	He can help us.
Dog:	But he's just a monkey!
Monkey:	I can so help!
Narrator:	There was almost a fight, but Momotaro calmed the animals down.
Momotaro:	Monkey, you may go. Here is a rice cake.

Momotaro, The Peach Boy *(cont.)*

Narrator:	On they went, with Momotaro walking between the dog and the monkey to keep them from fighting. They marched on and on, right to the edge of the wilderness. Suddenly, something flew out of the trees and landed in front of them. It was an enormous bird.
Bird:	Why are you here?
Momotaro:	I am on a trip.
Bird:	You are on my land.
Momotaro:	Yes, I am. But not for long.
Bird:	Give me some food or I will peck you.
Momotaro:	Oh no you won't.
Bird:	I won't?
Momotaro:	No. I am going to get rid of the demons.
Bird:	You are?
Momotaro:	Yes. I will give back the things they took from the people
Bird:	I am sorry I was rude. Please let me go with you.
Monkey:	NO!
Dog:	What? He can't go!
Momotaro:	He can help us.
Monkey:	No, he can't.
Dog:	He's just a bird!
Momotaro:	Stop fighting or I will send all of you home.
Narrator:	Momotaro's words quieted the animals down, for they all wanted to be a part of Momotaro's adventure.
Momotaro:	Bird, you may go, too. Here is a rice cake.
Narrator:	So the four companions traveled on toward the island of the demons. At last they came to the sea.
Dog:	I don't see the island.
Monkey:	I don't see it, either.

Momotaro, The Peach Boy (cont.)

Bird:	The sea is so big!
Momotaro:	What is the matter?
Dog:	We are afraid.
Momotaro:	Of what?
Monkey:	We are afraid of the sea.
Momotaro:	Then go on home.
Bird:	No! We want to stay with you!
Momotaro:	Then be quiet and help me. We have to make a boat.
Narrator:	Before long, they had their boat. They sailed toward the island of the demons. To mask their fears of the terribly rough sea, the animals did tricks.
Dog:	I can beg. See?
Monkey:	I can do flips. See?
Bird:	I can sing. See?
Momotaro:	There is the island. See?
Narrator:	Now, the island of the demons was a fearsome place with crooked black houses and dark narrow streets. At the very top of the island stood the demons' castle, surrounded by jagged rocks and burnt trees. The companions got out of the boat.
Dog, Monkey, and Bird:	What will we do now?
Momotaro:	Bird, you fly over the gate. See what the demon is doing and then come and tell us.
Narrator:	The bird was back in no time at all.
Bird:	He is on the roof.
Momotaro:	What did you say to him?
Bird:	I said, "Momotaro is here. Give up now."
Momotaro:	What did he do?
Bird:	He just laughed.

Momotaro, The Peach Boy *(cont.)*

Momotaro:	We will see about that!
Narrator:	Together the four companions went up the hill toward the demon's castle.
Momotaro:	Bird, you fly over the walls. Peck at the demon.
Bird:	I can do that.
Momotaro:	Monkey, you climb over the gate. Open it up.
Monkey:	I can do that.
Momotaro:	Dog, you be ready to bite him when he opens the gate.
Dog:	I can do that.
Narrator:	Momotaro's plan worked. After a fierce battle, Momotaro got the best of the demon.
Dog:	We won!
Monkey:	Hurray!
Bird:	Now what do we do?
Momotaro:	We will give the things they took to the people. Then we will go home.
Narrator:	And that is just what the companions did. The people of Japan were happy to have their riches returned and they made Momotaro a great hero. The animals went back to their homes. Momotaro went back to his parents, who were very glad to see the son they had found inside a peach.

The End

Momotaro, The Peach Boy

Mini-Lessons and Activities

- **Learning More about Short Vowels**

Place the following words from the story either on index cards or on a duplicated worksheet so that the children can cut the words apart to use. (am, an, and, at, back, can, that, glad, land beg, get, let, send, peck, tell, them, then, when, yes   rid, sing, big, him, flips, did, is, is, it, this, trip, will, with   dog, not, son, on, stop, won   but, cut just, up, us)   Also prepare either heading cards or duplicated pages with each vowel at the top of five columns:

A	E	I	O	U

Children may work in pairs to place the short vowel words under the correct vowel column. The teacher should check for understanding. The children can read the words aloud with their partner. They should be ready to tell why each word was placed under the appropriate vowel.

- Extension work

Make a KWL chart on Japan.

What we KNOW about Japan	What we WANT to know about Japan	What we LEARNED about Japan

- **Further Understanding of Text**

After the play has been performed, have the children choose to "be" one of the characters from Momotaro. Another child or the teacher will be a reporter. The reporter will interview the characters and ask them about their feelings and responses to particular events in the story. It would be fun for the children and the parents to videotape the interview and watch it later. Suggested parts: ogre, Momotaro, dog, monkey, bird, mother, father, peasants

- **Fluency—Chunking Phrases**

Select several of your favorite lines from the play. Copy these for an overhead transparency or write them on the board for the children to see. The teacher should model expressive reading of the lines aloud for the students. Do this modeling several times while the children listen and follow along. Talk about what you are doing to "put the words together like talking." You might block the phrases with your fingers as you read. Talk about how you are reading several words together in one breath. Discuss varying the speed of your reading. Show them how you emphasize particular words in the reading. Then have the children echo your reading (teacher reads, children repeat after the teacher). As a final fluency push, have the children actively read the lines as a choral reading.

The Old Hag's Long Leather Bag

A Story from Ireland

Multicultural Story Summary

In this tale, a hag steals a fortune from a widow and her daughters. The three daughters set out to find it, one by one. The first daughter meets the hag and begins to work for her. The hag tells her not to look up the chimney, but when the girl does, she sees the stolen bag. She takes it and runs past the hag's creatures, but refuses to help them. She gets to the mill, is caught by the hag, and turned into a stone. The second daughter meets the same fate. The third daughter is kinder, though, and after she takes back the bag, she helps the hag's creatures. They help her in turn when the hag comes after her. The mill dumps the hag into the stream, tells the girl to touch the stones with the hag's magic stick, and the three sisters are reunited. They return home with the bag of gold and silver.

Suggested Props

two rocks, a loaf of bread, a bag of gold, stick

Setting

There are two poor cottages at the far ends of the stage.

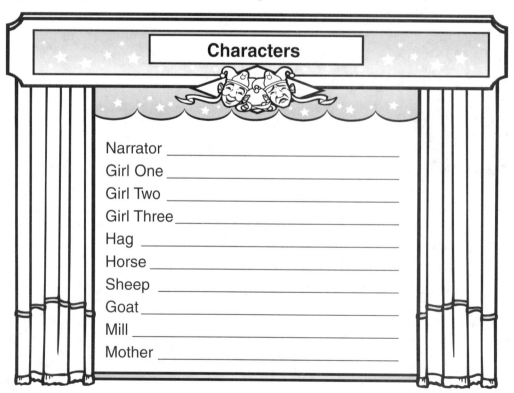

Characters

Narrator _____

Girl One _____

Girl Two _____

Girl Three _____

Hag _____

Horse _____

Sheep _____

Goat _____

Mill _____

Mother _____

The Old Hag's Long Leather Bag (cont.)

Word List

a	girls	is	our	time
again	give	it	out	to
all	glad	it's	please	too
am	go	jewels	poor	touch
and	goat	just	put	turn
anyway	going	keep	rich	turned
are	gold	know	right	two
back	gone	leather	rocks	up
bag	good	like	rub	very
be	grass	long	rubbed	was
been	ha	look	see	way
bread	had	luck	she	we
but	hag's	lucky	sheep	well
by	happy	maid	silver	wend
bye	harder	me	since	we're
chimney	has	mill	sleeping	what
closer	hasn't	mine	some	wheel
come	have	mother	somewhere	where
course	haven't	must	soon	why
cut	hello	my	stay	will
dear	help	need	stick	with
did	here	never	take	wool
do	hey	new	takes	work
doing	hmmm	no	tell	world
easy	home	not	thank	would
eat	horse	now	that	yes
else	house	of	the	you
find	I	oh	them	your
food	if	okay	there	
get	in	on	they	
girl	inside	one	think	

The Old Hag's Long Leather Bag

Narrator:	Long ago, in far off Ireland, there lived a mother and her three daughters. Before the father had died, he had given them a long leather bag brimming with gold and silver and jewels. It wasn't long before an evil woman came around and heard of the fortune. She decided to steal the bag of riches for herself.
Hag:	Ha, ha! I have the bag! I am rich!
Narrator:	When the mother went to get some money from the bag, she discovered it was gone.
Mother:	Oh, dear! The bag is gone! What will we do?
Girl One:	Oh, no! We are poor!
Girl Two:	Oh, no! We will have no food to eat!
Girl Three:	It's okay. We will just have to work harder.
Narrator:	And so they did, but it was very difficult to support four people on nothing. They decided one of them had to go out into the world and find a way to make money.
Girl One:	I will go find my way in the world.
Mother:	Okay.
Girl One:	Mother, will you give me some bread?
Mother:	Yes, I will. Here you are.
Girl One:	Thank you. If I am not back soon, you will know I have been lucky.
Mother:	Very well.
Mother, Girl Two, and Girl Three:	Good bye! Good luck!
Narrator:	The girl walked until she was in a new town. She was tired of searching. She came upon an old house by the side of the road. Now, it just so happened that the woman who owned this house was really the hag who'd stolen their family fortune.
Hag:	Hello there, girl.
Girl One:	Hello.
Hag:	What are you doing here?
Girl One:	I am going to find my way in the world.
Hag:	Would you like to stay here? I need a maid.
Girl One:	What would I do?
Hag:	You will help me. You will keep house.
Girl One:	That is easy.

The Old Hag's Long Leather Bag *(cont.)*

Hag:	It is. But you are NEVER to look up the chimney. NEVER!
Girl One:	All right.
Narrator:	The next day, the girl helped the old woman clean the house.
Hag:	I have to go out now.
Girl One:	Okay. Good bye.
Narrator:	Now that she was all alone, the girl's curiosity got the better of her.
Girl One:	Now why did she tell me to not look up the chimney?
Narrator:	She bent over and looked up the chimney. And what do you suppose she found hidden there?
Girl One:	It is our bag of gold and silver and jewels!
Narrator:	She snatched the long leather bag from its hiding place in the chimney and began running down the road towards her home. She hadn't gone too far when she came upon a horse grazing in a field.
Horse:	Girl, please come rub me.
Girl One:	What?
Horse:	I haven't been rubbed in a very long time.
Girl One:	Get out of my way!
Narrator:	And she pushed the horse out of her way with a stick. She went on and soon met a sheep.
Sheep:	Girl, please come cut my wool.
Girl One:	What?
Sheep:	I haven't had my wool cut in a very long time.
Girl One:	Get out of my way!
Narrator:	She struck out at the sheep and went on down the road. There she met a goat.
Goat:	Girl, please come put me over there on some new grass.
Girl One:	What?
Goat:	I haven't been put out on new grass in a very long time.
Narrator:	She waved her stick under the goat's nose and went along until she came to a mill.
Girl One:	Get out of my way!
Mill:	Girl, please come turn my wheel.
Girl One:	What?

The Old Hag's Long Leather Bag *(cont.)*

Mill:	I haven't had my wheel turned in a very long time.
Narrator:	But the girl paid no attention. She went inside the mill, put the long leather bag under her head as a pillow and fell asleep. In the meantime, the old hag had returned home.
Hag:	Oh, me. I am happy to be home. I need help. Girl!
Narrator:	There was no answer. Then the hag noticed the girl's things were gone. Suspecting the worst, she looked up the chimney.
Hag:	The bag is gone!
Narrator:	Gathering up her magic stick, she stormed out of the house. She went down the road until she met up with the horse.
Hag:	Horse, did you see a girl go by?
Horse:	Yes, I did.
Hag:	Did she have a long leather bag?
Horse:	Yes, she did.
Hag:	Has it been long since she went by?
Horse:	No, it hasn't.
Narrator:	The old woman went on until she came upon the sheep.
Hag:	Sheep, did you see a girl go by?
Sheep:	Yes, I did.
Hag:	Did she have a long leather bag?
Sheep:	Yes, she did.
Hag:	Has it been long since she went by?
Sheep:	No, it hasn't.
Narrator:	The old crone huffed and puffed on down the road. There stood the goat.
Hag:	Goat, did you see a girl go by?
Goat:	Yes, I did.
Hag:	Did she have a long leather bag?
Goat:	Yes, she did.
Hag:	Has it been long since she went by?
Goat:	No, it hasn't.
Narrator:	On the hag stomped until she came to the mill.
Hag:	Mill, did you see a girl go by?
Mill:	Yes. She is sleeping inside.

The Old Hag's Long Leather Bag *(cont.)*

Hag:	Is she!?
Narrator:	The hag went in and touched the sleeping girl with the magic stick. This turned the girl into stone. The hag picked up the precious bag and went on home.
Hag:	That was mine, anyway.
Narrator:	Meanwhile, time passed on by. The mother and the two daughters hadn't heard a word from the oldest girl.
Mother:	She must have been lucky.
Girl Two:	I think I will go into the world and find my way, too.
Mother:	Okay.
Girl Two:	Will you give me some bread?
Mother:	Yes, I will. Here you are.
Girl Two:	Thank you. If I am not back soon, you will know I have been lucky.
Mother:	Very well.
Mother and Girl Three:	Good bye! Good luck!
Narrator:	The second daughter just so happened to take the very same road as her older sister. When she got tired of walking, she looked around. There was a little house and it belonged to the hag.
Hag:	Hello there.
Girl Two:	Hello.
Hag:	What are you doing here?
Girl Two:	I am going to find my way in the world.
Hag:	Would you like to stay here? I need a maid.
Girl Two:	What would I do?
Hag:	You will help me keep house.
Girl Two:	That is easy.
Hag:	It is. But you are NEVER to look up the chimney. NEVER!
Girl Two:	All right.
Narrator:	But the very next day, the old woman left the house for a little walk. The girl could not resist peeking up into the chimney.
Girl Two:	Hey! It is our bag of gold and silver and jewels!

The Old Hag's Long Leather Bag *(cont.)*

Narrator: Off she ran with the valuable bag over her shoulder. She headed for home. She hadn't gone too far when she came upon the horse.

Horse: Girl, please come rub me.

Girl Two: What?

Horse: I haven't been rubbed in a very long time.

Girl Two: Get out of my way!

Narrator: Rudely, she pushed the poor horse out of her way. On she went until she met a sheep.

Sheep: Girl, please come cut my wool.

Girl Two: What?

Sheep: I haven't had my wool cut in a very long time.

Girl Two: Get out of my way!

Narrator: She shoved the poor sheep out of her way. Then she went along the road. She met the goat.

Goat: Girl, please come put me over there on some new grass.

Girl Two: What?

Goat: I haven't been put on new grass in a very long time.

Girl Two: Get out of my way!

Narrator: And the goat was bumped aside, too. Soon, the girl came to the mill.

Mill: Girl, please come turn my wheel.

Girl Two: What?

Mill: I haven't had my wheel turned in a very long time.

Narrator: The girl paid absolutely no attention and went inside the mill to rest. She put the long leather bag filled with her family's fortune under her head. Then she fell fast asleep. Meanwhile, the hag returned to her little house.

Hag: Oh, me. I am glad to be home. I need some help. Girl!

Narrator: Of course, the girl didn't come when the hag called. The hag went looking for her and found that the girl's things were gone. She immediately looked up the chimney into her secret hiding place.

Hag: My bag is gone!

Narrator: She was furious! Down the road she stormed with her magic stick in her hand. She came to the horse.

The Old Hag's Long Leather Bag (cont.)

Hag:	Horse, did you see a girl go by?
Horse:	Yes, I did.
Hag:	Did she have a long leather bag?
Horse:	Yes, she did.
Hag:	Has it been long since she went by?
Horse:	No, it hasn't.
Narrator:	Fuming, the hag went on down the road. She came to the sheep.
Hag:	Sheep, did you see a girl go by?
Sheep:	Yes, I did.
Hag:	Did she have a long leather bag?
Sheep:	Yes, she did.
Hag:	Has it been long since she went by?
Sheep:	No, it hasn't.
Narrator:	On and on she went, puffing down the road. Soon she came upon the goat.
Hag:	Goat, did you see a girl go by?
Goat:	Yes, I did.
Hag:	Did she have a long leather bag?
Goat:	Yes, she did.
Hag:	Has it been long since she went by?
Goat:	No, it hasn't.
Narrator:	And then the hag came to the mill.
Hag:	Mill, did you see a girl go by?
Mill:	Yes. She is sleeping inside.
Hag:	Is she?!
Narrator:	The hag crept in and touched the girl with her magic stick. The girl turned to stone. Now two stones lay inside the mill. Picking up the precious bag, the hag made her way back home.
Hag:	No one takes my bag!
Narrator:	Well, more time passed on by. The mother and the youngest daughter had not heard from either girl.
Mother:	My girls must be doing well. They must be rich.

The Old Hag's Long Leather Bag *(cont.)*

Girl Three:	I will go, too. I will find my way in the world.
Mother:	Okay.
Girl Three:	Will you give me some bread?
Mother:	Yes, I will. Here you are.
Girl Three:	Thank you.
Mother:	Good bye! Good luck!
Narrator:	So the third girl traveled on the same road her sisters had used. It was just luck that she came upon the old woman who had stolen their bag of riches. Of course, she couldn't have known that this woman had the long leather bag when they began to talk.
Hag:	Hello there.
Girl Three:	Hello.
Hag:	What are you doing here?
Girl Three:	I am going to find my way in the world.
Hag:	Would you like to stay here? I need a maid.
Girl Three:	What would I do?
Hag:	You will help me keep house.
Girl Three:	That is easy.
Hag: It is.	But you are NEVER to look up the chimney. NEVER!
Girl Three:	All right.
Narrator:	Not long after that, the hag wanted to leave the house to do some errands.
Hag:	I have to go out now.
Girl Three:	Okay.
Narrator:	As you might imagine, the girl couldn't help but look up the chimney the very second the hag was out of sight.
Girl Three:	It is our bag of gold and silver and jewels!
Narrator:	She pulled the bag from its hiding place, flung it over her shoulder, and ran from the house. She hadn't gone far when she came upon the horse.
Horse:	Girl, please come rub me.
Girl Three:	What?
Horse:	I haven't been rubbed in a very long time.
Girl Three:	Poor horse. Of course I will rub you.

The Old Hag's Long Leather Bag (cont.)

Narrator:	The horse was very thankful to have a rub after all that time. The girl went on down the road until she met the sheep.
Sheep:	Girl, please come cut my wool.
Girl Three:	What?
Sheep:	I haven't had my wool cut in a very long time.
Girl Three:	Poor sheep. Of course I will cut your wool.
Narrator:	And she did. The sheep was happy to be rid of all that wool. The girl went along until she met the goat.
Goat:	Girl, please put me over there on some new grass.
Girl Three:	What?
Goat:	I haven't been put on some new grass in a very long time.
Girl Three:	Of course I will put you on some new grass.
Narrator:	Naturally, the goat was delighted to have some fresh green grass to eat. After she helped the goat, the girl went on her way until she got to the mill.
Mill:	Girl, please come turn my wheel.
Girl Three:	What?
Mill:	I haven't had my wheel turned in a very long time.
Girl Three:	Poor mill. Of course I will turn your wheel.
Narrator:	The mill was very happy to be working again. The girl went inside and fell asleep with the precious bag under her head. Meanwhile, back at the hag's house, the mean old lady had returned from her chore.
Hag:	Oh, me. I am happy to be home. Girl!
Narrator:	There was no answer. Having been fooled twice, the hag peered up the chimney.
Hag:	Not again! My bag is gone!
Narrator:	She hobbled from the house as fast as she could and went down the road. Soon she met the horse.
Hag:	Horse, did you see a girl go by?
Horse:	No. Go look somewhere else.
Hag:	Hmmmm.
Narrator:	Then she came upon the sheep.
Hag:	Sheep, did you see a girl go by?
Sheep:	No. Go look somewhere else.

The Old Hag's Long Leather Bag *(cont.)*

Hag: Hmmmm.

Narrator: On she went until she came upon the goat.

Hag: Goat, did you see a girl go by?

Goat: No. Go look somewhere else.

Hag: Hmmmm.

Narrator: At last she came to the old mill.

Hag: Mill, did you see a girl go by?

Mill: Come closer.

Hag: What?

Mill: Come closer. I will tell you where she is.

Narrator: So the hag unwisely came closer. The mill grabbed her up and tossed her in the water. As she fell, she lost hold of the magic stick. The mill pushed her down the river. The hag's screams woke the girl.

Mill: Girl!

Girl Three: Yes?

Mill: Take the hag's stick.

Girl Three: Okay.

Mill: Go inside.

Girl Three: Okay.

Mill: There are two rocks inside.

Girl Three: Yes, I see them.

Mill: Touch them with the hag's stick.

Girl Three: Oh!

Narrator: Just like that, the hag's magic spell was broken! The three sisters went back to their home as fast as they could, sharing the weight of the long leather bag between them.

Mother: My girls!

All Girls: Mother! We're home!

Narrator: The wealth from the long leather bag lasted the rest of their lives, which they spent happily ever after.

The End

The Old Hag's Long Leather Bag *(cont.)*

Mini-Lessons and Activities

- **Characters in Folk Tales**

  Explain to the class that we know from the very beginning of a folk tale who is going to be a "good" character and who is a "bad" character. Tell the children that characters often don't grow and change in fairy tales and folk tales like they do in novels. Readers can predict what the characters will do, how they will speak, act, and why they do what they do. We enjoy knowing how predictable they are—and we like knowing what they will do next. Use familiar examples for other literature to help them understand this concept in a class discussion.

  To help children understand stereotypical fairy tale characters, you might begin with a chart:

Characteristics	Little Red Riding Hood	Cinderella	The Old Hag's Long Leather Bag
3rd Child (might be lazy or silly, but wins the day due to a kind heart or cleverness)			
Father (boastful or proud)			
Mother (sometimes dies and returns as a helpful animal)			
Step-mother (often cruel)			
Mentor (helps out)			
Kind Animals (helps out in return for a kindness)			
Wicked Animals (threaten the main character			

Use the chart to learn more about folk tale characters. Compare the characters in several stories the children know to another familiar tale.

The Prawn That Caused Trouble

A Story from Myanmar

Multicultural Story Summary

One careless move causes a chain reaction in the animal world. The man almost steps on the prawn (shrimp); the prawn bites the man; the man hits the tree; the tree drops fruit on a rooster; the rooster scratches dirt on an ant; the ant stings the snake; the snake bites the pig; the pig knocks down the banana tree, which is the bat's home; the bat bites the elephant; the elephant kicks a rock; and the rock crushes the lady's house. The lady tries to find who is to blame. Everyone blames the next characters until they come to the prawn. The man decides to cook the prawn into soup, but the toad eats the prawn before the soup is finished. The man rebuilds the house and replants the tree.

Setting

There is a house in a forest. A river runs in front of the house.

Suggested Props

fishing pole, pot, water

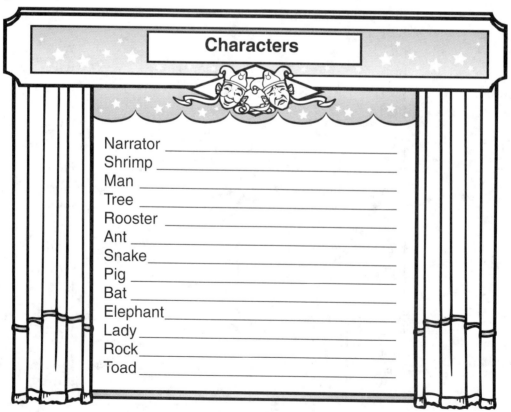

Characters

Narrator _____
Shrimp _____
Man _____
Tree _____
Rooster _____
Ant _____
Snake _____
Pig _____
Bat _____
Elephant _____
Lady _____
Rock _____
Toad _____

The Prawn That Caused Trouble *(cont.)*

Word List

a	fault	money	teach
about	fell	move	tell
all	first	my	that
am	fix	need	the
an	for	no	there
and	fruit	not	think
anything	give	of	this
anyway	go	oh	threw
at	going	on	to
ate	ground	or	toad
banana	have	ow	too
bat's	he	pay	tree
be	help	pig	want
bit	here	pig's	was
blame	hey	place	wasn't
but	hill	please	water
can	him	pool	way
catch	hit	prawn	we
caused	hot	problem	well
chance	house	right	were
close	hurt	rooster	what
cold	I	should	what's
come	I'll	shrimp	when
cook	in	snake	where
cooked	into	so	who
course	is	some	why
did	it	son	will
didn't	just	sorry	work
do	kicked	soup	wrong
don't	lady	step	yes
down	like	stop	you
drink	lot	stung	your
elephant	man	talk	
everyone	me	tasted	

The Prawn That Caused the Trouble

Narrator:	Once upon a time in a far-off land called Myanmar, a man was getting ready to fish in the river. He waded into the water, taking very little care about where he was walking. The man narrowly missed crushing a little prawn or shrimp that lived in the river.
Shrimp:	Hey! Stop! You will step on me!
Narrator:	The man didn't hear the tiny shrimp's voice, so the prawn bit the man's leg.
Man:	Ow! That hurt!
Shrimp:	There! That will teach you to come too close to me!
Man:	What was that? What bit me?
Narrator:	The man didn't see a thing in the water, so he hit a nearby tree in his frustration.
Tree:	Hey! Why hit ME? What did I do?
Narrator:	And the tree dropped a huge fruit from its branches, hoping to hit the man on the head. But the fruit missed the man and hit an innocent rooster.
Rooster:	Hey! That hurt! What is going on here?
Narrator:	The rooster almost attacked the tree, but instead, took out his anger on an ant nest. He scratched dirt over the little creatures, who were minding their own business.
Rooster:	There! You like to work! Well, work on that!
Ant:	Hey! We have a lot of work to do! Don't do that!
Narrator:	And in retaliation, the ant stung a snake.
Snake:	Hey! That hurt! And what was that for?
Narrator:	The busy ant didn't answer, so the snake went after a wild pig. The snake gave the pig a bite on the tail.
Pig:	Hey! That hurt! Why did you do that?
Snake:	The ant stung me.
Pig:	So what? I am not an ant. I am a pig!
Snake:	You were there, that's all.

The Prawn That Caused the Trouble *(cont.)*

Narrator:	The wild pig stormed off to dig up a banana tree, which happened to be home to the bat.
Bat:	Hey! What's going on down there?
Narrator:	Bat didn't see the pig under the tree, but he DID see Elephant. He flew down and bit the elephant's ear.
Elephant:	Hey! That hurt! Why did you do that?
Narrator:	Elephant kicked over a rock, which rolled down a hill and flattened a house belonging to a little old lady. Luckily, she wasn't hurt. But she WAS furious!
Lady:	Hey! That was my house!
Rock:	So what?
Lady:	I'll tell you what . . . . You have to pay for the house. I have to have a house!
Rock:	No way! Elephant kicked me down that hill. He should pay.
Lady:	What?
Rock:	Your house was in the wrong place, anyway.
Lady:	What!
Narrator:	The old lady ran up the hill and faced Elephant.
Lady:	Hey! You need to pay for my house!
Elephant:	Oh, no. I will not do that!
Lady:	What?
Elephant:	It was all bat's fault.
Bat:	My fault?!?
Elephant:	Yes, it was!
Bat:	But my house fell to the ground! Everyone should help ME! Go talk to the banana tree!
Tree:	Me? It is pig's fault. Here I am on the ground. Why not help ME?

The Prawn That Caused the Trouble *(cont.)*

Lady:	Stop it! What about my house? Who will fix it?
Narrator:	The old lady saw the pig and chased after him.
Lady:	Hey, pig! Give me money to fix my house!
Pig:	Not a chance. Blame the snake. He bit ME!
Lady:	Snake?!
Narrator:	So she went after Snake.
Lady:	Snake! Pay for my house.
Snake:	What? It wasn't me. Blame the ant. He stung me.
Lady:	Don't move! I will talk to the ant.
Narrator:	And so that is what she did.
Lady:	Ant, you will pay for my house!
Ant:	Don't blame me. Blame the rooster.
Lady:	The rooster?
Ant:	That's right.
Narrator:	She looked at the rooster.
Lady:	Rooster! Fix my house!
Rooster:	Talk to the tree, lady. He threw fruit at me. And I didn't do anything to him.
Lady:	Tree, is that so?
Tree:	Me? Blame that man. He hit me first.
Narrator:	The lady looked at the man.
Lady:	Well, that is my son. He will fix my house.
Man:	Of course I will. But first I will catch this prawn. HE caused the problem.
Shrimp:	Who? ME?
All:	Yes! You!
Man:	You should be cooked!
Shrimp:	What?!?

The Prawn That Caused the Trouble *(cont.)*

Man:	Well, do you want to be cooked in cold water or in hot water?
Narrator:	Shrimp gulped. To be honest, he preferred neither!
Shrimp:	Cold water, please.
Narrator:	The prawn swam to the bottom of the cold pool. He laughed and laughed. He had escaped being eaten for the main course of dinner. The man didn't think the prawn's behavior was very funny. He wanted to get even.
Man:	Hey, Elephant! Drink the water in the pool!
Narrator:	And the elephant did just that.
Lady:	Give the shrimp to Toad.
Man:	Why do that?
Lady:	He can cook it into soup.
Narrator:	And that is what happened.
Toad:	Come and have some soup!
Narrator:	The group sat down to enjoy the soup.
Pig:	Hey! This is just water!
Rooster:	Where is the shrimp?
Toad:	Oh! I am sorry! I think I ate the shrimp when I tasted the soup!
Narrator:	Everyone was so angry at Toad that they pinched his back—which is why toads have warts to this day. The man rebuilt his mother's house and replanted the banana tree. And although the soup was a disappointment, every one had had an interesting day—except for the poor prawn. No one really cared what he thought!

The End

The Prawn That Caused Trouble (cont.)

Mini-Lessons and Activities

- **Classification**

Discuss the difference between "true" and "not true." Use a chart similar to the one below to help the children organize their thoughts. They may work with a partner to find incidents in the story that could be true and events that are not true. (The class might also be divided into teams to find events from the play.) The children will need to justify their choices and conclusions.

THINGS THAT COULD BE TRUE	THINGS THAT COULD NOT BE TRUE
Example: A shrimp could live in a river.	Example: Animals cannot talk.

- **Word Study**

Beginning readers may have trouble understanding, hearing, or inventing rhymes. Explain that rhyming words do not have the same onset letter (beginning letter), but they sometimes have the same rime (ending cluster of letters). Use magnetic letters to show the children this principle.

Magnetic letters: a n

Letters to be used at the onset letter: m p c f t

Explain that you will use one of the beginning letters and add it to /an/ to make a new word. Using the magnetic letters, show the children what you mean. Take off the onset letter and use a new letter. Have the children read the new word, as well as the previously formed word. When the children demonstrate understanding, give them the opportunity to think of their own rhymes. Make their words with the magnetic letters.

Use these words from the play. The children may work in pairs to generate rhymes.

Words to use: bat, pig, will, old, me, and, stop, in, it, cook

The words the children generate do not have to be from the play.

- **Comprehension**

This particular play is written in a circular form—that is, all the events are connected in a cause and effect cycle. Have the children draw a picture of each character in the play. Then link the characters with large, puffy arrows to show which character caused the next character to react.

Write verbs on the linking arrows to show what action the character took. For example, the shrimp BIT the man. Write the word BIT on the arrow that connects the shrimp to the man.

Post the children's display with the title of the play written inside the circle made by the characters and their linking arrows. Have the children retell the story using their huge diagram!

Tricky Mr. Rabbit

A Story from Africa

Multicultural Story Summary

Tricky Mr. Rabbit decides to trick the elephant. He tells the elephants that he, the rabbit, is strong enough to pull him. Rabbit ties a rope to Elephant. Then he tricks a whale into a pulling contest. Instead of the rabbit pulling, the huge beasts are actually pulling each other until they discover the truth. Elephants runs after Rabbit, but Rabbit hides in a skull. He speaks to Elephant as if he was a dead rabbit and tricks him once again.

Setting

on a beach

Suggested Props

rope, skull

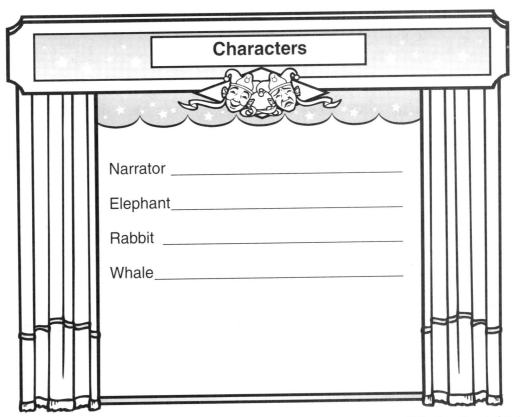

Characters

Narrator _____

Elephant_____

Rabbit _____

Whale_____

Tricky Mr. Rabbit *(cont.)*

Word List

a	go	on	to
about	good	other	today
after	ha	paw	too
again	have	play	trick
all	he	please	tricking
am	here	pointed	tricks
an	hey	pull	trip
and	him	pulling	try
animals	his	rabbit	turned
are	home	right	untie
around	hope	rope	up
as	how	rude	us
at	I	said	very
be	if	sea	walk
been	into	see	was
bet	is	seen	wasn't
big	land	sit	way
but	like	still	we
by	little	stop	well
bye	look	stopping	were
can	love	strong	whale
catch	luck	talking	what
closer	may	tell	where
come	me	that	why
did	myself	the	will
don't	never	then	with
down	no	think	won't
elephant	not	this	would
end	nothing	tickle	wow
feet	now	tickled	yes
for	oh	tie	you
get	okay	time	yours

Tricky Mr. Rabbit

Narrator:	Long ago, on a continent called Africa, there lived a little rabbit who loved playing tricks. He especially loved playing tricks on animals much, much larger than himself.
Rabbit:	Yes! I love to play tricks on the big animals!
Narrator:	One day, Mr. Rabbit was taking a stroll on the beach when he came upon Mr. Elephant.
Rabbit:	Wow! You are big!
Elephant:	Yes, I am.
Rabbit:	You have big feet!
Elephant:	Well, yes, I do.
Rabbit:	I have never seen feet as big as yours!
Narrator:	The elephant frowned. The rabbit, after all, was being a bit rude.
Rabbit:	I bet you can not walk well with big feet like that.
Elephant:	What?
Rabbit:	I bet you trip all the time with feet that big.
Elephant:	How rude! I think you need to be tickled.
Rabbit:	Ha, ha!
Narrator:	The rabbit laughed and hopped around the elephant in a big circle. The time was right to begin tricking the elephant.
Rabbit:	I think I will tie this rope around you! I think I will pull you right into the sea!
Elephant:	What! You think you can pull me into the sea?
Rabbit:	Yes, I think I can.
Elephant:	No way, little rabbit.
Narrator:	The rabbit picked up some rope which just so happened to be on the beach.
Rabbit:	We will see.
Elephant:	Okay, we will.
Rabbit:	I will tie this rope around you.
Elephant:	Okay.
Rabbit:	If I can not pull you into the sea, then you may tickle me. And I will sit still as you tickle me, too.
Elephant:	All right. Go on.

Tricky Mr. Rabbit *(cont.)*

Narrator:	So the rabbit tied the rope around the elephant's middle. He ran far down the beach holding the old end of the rope. Before long, he couldn't see the elephant, but he COULD see a whale in the ocean.
Rabbit:	Hey! Whale!
Whale:	Yes.
Rabbit:	You are big.
Whale:	Yes, I am.
Rabbit:	I am little.
Whale:	Yes, you are.
Rabbit:	I think I can pull you up on the land.
Whale:	What? You think you can pull me up on the land?
Rabbit:	Yes, I think I can.
Whale:	No way!
Rabbit:	We will see.
Whale:	Okay, we will.
Rabbit:	I will tie this rope around you.
Whale:	I have nothing to do today. You can try, little rabbit.
Rabbit:	Good!
Narrator:	So the rabbit tied the rope around the whale. Mr. Rabbit tried not to laugh right out loud as he worked.
Rabbit:	Now, you pull on this end.
Whale:	Okay.
Rabbit:	I will pull on the other end.
Whale:	All right.
Narrator:	Mr. Rabbit hopped off to tease the elephant. The whale started to swim out to sea.
Rabbit:	Elephant! Oh, Elephant! I am now going to pull you into the sea!
Elephant:	Ha!
Rabbit:	See if you can stop me!
Narrator:	Just then, the elephant felt a very strong tug on the rope.
Elephant:	Wow! The little rabbit is strong!
Narrator:	The elephant pulled as hard as he could. But try as he might, he couldn't budge the rabbit. In fact, he was having a bit of trouble just staying in one place. Meanwhile, the whale was having the same kind of problem.

Tricky Mr. Rabbit (cont.)

Whale:	Wow! The little rabbit is strong!
Narrator:	Mr. Rabbit was hiding behind a clump of sea grapes having a good laugh.
Rabbit:	Ha, ha! What a good trick!
Narrator:	Both huge animals were getting more puzzled by the minute.
Whale:	How is that little rabbit stopping me?
Narrator:	The whale flipped its tail flukes and went further out into the ocean. The elephant was pulled closer to the water, little by little.
Elephant:	Hey! How can that little rabbit pull me?
Narrator:	Finally, the elephant's feet were in the salty water. He turned around. Now he could see the rope was tied around a great whale and not the little rabbit.
Elephant:	Whale! Have you been talking to a little rabbit?
Narrator:	The whale looked around and saw an elephant, not a rabbit, tied to the other end of the rope.
Whale:	Why, yes, I have. Why are you pulling the rope? The rabbit said he would pull.
Elephant:	This is a trick. Come closer. I will untie the rope.
Whale:	Okay. I will do that.
Narrator:	While they were being untied, the rabbit dried his tears of laughter and scampered off. At last, the huge animals were free of the rope.
Elephant:	That rabbit! I will catch him. I will tickle him for tricking us!
Whale:	Good luck. I hope you get him.
fNarrator:	The elephant ran off as fast as his big feet would carry him.
Elephant:	I will catch you, rabbit!
Narrator:	Soon, the elephant WAS catching up to the rabbit. When the rabbit realized that, he quickly hid inside an old skull which was on the sand. He had to catch his breath and think of what to do next. The elephant stopped right by the skull and scratched his head.
.Elephant:	Where is that rabbit?
Narrator:	Tricky Mr. Rabbit saw another chance to fool the elephant. He disguised his voice.
Rabbit:	Here I am!
Elephant:	Where?
Rabbit:	Look down here.

Tricky Mr. Rabbit *(cont.)*

Elephant:	Where?
Rabbit:	Here!
Narrator:	The elephant looked down at the skull. He was puzzled.
Elephant:	Have you seen a little rabbit go by?
Rabbit:	Yes, I have. But then, I was an elephant.
Elephant:	You were?
Rabbit:	Yes. That rabbit was very rude, wasn't he?
Elephant:	Yes, he was.
Rabbit:	I was about to tickle him myself.
Elephant:	You were?
Rabbit:	Yes. And then he pointed his paw at me.
Elephant:	He did?
Rabbit:	Yes. He turned me into THIS!
Elephant:	No way!
Rabbit:	Oh, yes, he did.
Narrator:	The elephant became frightened. He didn't want to become a pile of dry old bones.
Elephant:	Well, if you see him again, please don't tell him I was after him.
Rabbit:	Okay. I won't tell him.
Elephant:	Don't tell him that you have seen me at all. I think I will go home now.
Rabbit:	All right. Good bye.
Narrator:	As soon as the elephant was safely out of sight, the rabbit crawled out of the skull. Then he hopped towards his own home, laughing hysterically. All in all, it had been a great day for tricks!

The End

Tricky Mr. Rabbit *(cont.)*

Mini-Lessons and Activities

- **Word Study**

Display the following consonant clusters found in this selection:

PL   TH   ST   TR   WH

The students can work in small groups to locate words in the text that begins with these consonant clusters. Record their findings on a chart.

As an extension activity, have the students come up with words they know beginning with these clusters. These additional words do not need to be located in the story.

Record these words on a chart to review at a later date as a word study activity.

- **Comprehension**

Show the students a story map from a previous story or model the development of a story map from a story all the children are familiar with, such as Cinderella.

As a group, discuss the sequence of important events in Tricky Mr. Rabbit. Make a list of these events so the students may use them to design their own story maps. Children may work singly or in pairs or small groups to develop a story map for Tricky Mr. Rabbit. Give them the opportunity to share their maps and explain their work to the class.

The story map may also be used as a comprehension check as the child retells the story from his/her work.

- **Character Traits**

Help the students generate a list of character traits. Traits could include such words as: evil, kind, happy, sad, helpful, lazy, clever, etc.

The teacher can then prepare a semantic grid showing the characters' names and the character traits the children generated. If low vocabulary is an issue, the teacher can prepare the chart ahead of time and explain the meanings of the words she wishes to use.

Character	Happy	Clever	Gullible	Helpful	Evil
Mr. Rabbit					
Elephant					
Whale					

The students place an /x/ in the box that describes the character. More than one trait may be checked. The students must justify their answers from examples in the text.

Lazy Jack

A Story from England

Multicultural Story Summary

Jack is a lazy boy who hires himself out to the neighboring farmer. Jack earns rewards from the farmer. However, each time he is given a reward, he takes advice literally and spoils his reward. He earns money, but he drops it in the stream. His mother tells him to put his reward in his pocket next time. So he does, but this time, he has earned a jug of milk. He puts it in his pocket and it spills out. His mother tells him that next time he should carry his reward on his head. Jack earns a cheese, which he puts on his head, but it melts by the time he gets home. His mother tells him to carry his reward in his hands. Jack earns a kitten next. But the kitten doesn't like being carried in his hands, claws him, and runs away. The mother tells Jack to tie a string around his reward and pull it. Jack does this to a chunk of meat. Of course, it gets dirty in the road. Mother tells him to carry his reward on his back. But the next day, Jack is given a donkey. He puts it on his back. He walks by a castle where a sad princess lives. By making a sad princess laugh, he finally does the right thing and is rewarded by marrying the princess.

Setting

On one side of the stage, there is a poor cottage. On the other, there is a castle. Between them is a farm.

Suggested Props

coins, jug or jar, cheese, stuffed kitten, two crowns, string, meat, donkey

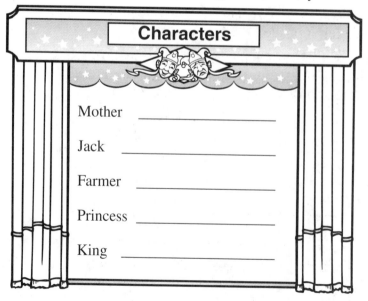

Characters

Mother _____

Jack _____

Farmer _____

Princess _____

King _____

Lazy Jack *(cont.)*

Word List

a	find	like	should
all	for	look	so
and	funny	made	some
are	go	make	someone
around	good	marry	spilled
back	ha	me	string
be	hands	meat	sun
behind	hard	melted	thank
boy	has	milk	that
but	have	money	the
can	he	mother	then
carried	head	my	time
catch	here	next	to
cheese	him	now	too
cold	his	of	very
daughter	hot	oh	water
dear	I	okay	we
did	if	on	well
didn't	in	pocket	what
dirty	is	pulled	where
do	it	put	will
doing	job	rich	work
donkey	jug	right	yes
down	kitten	road	you
dragged	laugh	sad	your
dropped	laughed	scratched	
farmer	let	see	

Lazy Jack

Narrator:	Once upon a time in a country called England, there was a lazy boy named Jack. Jack lived with this mother in a poor cottage.
Mother:	Oh, dear me!
Jack:	What is it, Mother?
Mother:	We have to have some money.
Jack:	Oh, we do?
Mother:	Yes, you have to find work.
Jack:	Oh, I do?
Mother:	Yes! Go on! Find a job!
Narrator:	She pointed to the door and down the road.
Mother:	See that farmer?
Jack:	Yes, I see him.
Mother:	He will have a job for you.
Jack:	Oh, dear me.
Narrator:	Jack went down the road to speak with the farmer about a job when he really just wanted to take a nap.
Farmer:	I do have work for you.
Jack:	Good.
Narrator:	Jack worked hard all day in the farmer's yard. He raked and pulled weeds and planted flowers.
Farmer:	Here is some money for all your work.
Jack:	Thank you!
Narrator:	Jack walked toward home. But on the way, he accidentally dropped the coins into a stream. He knew he'd be in trouble with his mother. Jack searched for the coins, but he was unable to find them. Sadly and slowly, he went on home.
Mother:	Do you have money?
Jack:	Well, I DID have money.
Mother:	Well, where is the money?
Jack:	I dropped it in the water.

Lazy Jack *(cont.)*

Mother:	What? You should have put the money in your pocket.
Jack:	You are right. Next time, I will do that.
Narrator:	The next day, Jack walked back to the farmer's house to look for work.
Farmer:	I do have work for you.
Jack:	Good.
Narrator:	Jack worked hard all day in the barn. He milked cows and fed the sheep.
Farmer:	Here is a jug of good, cold milk for all your work.
Jack:	Thank you.
Narrator:	Remembering his mother's advice, Jack put the jug of milk into his pocket and started home. But on the way, the milk spilled down his pants leg and onto the road. Jack knew he would be in trouble.
Mother:	Do you have money?
Jack:	No. But I have milk.
Mother:	Well, where is the milk?
Jack:	It spilled in the road.
Mother:	You should have carried it on your head.
Jack:	You are right. Next time, I will do that.
Narrator:	The next day, Jack got another job from the kind farmer.
Farmer:	I do have work for you.
Jack:	Good.
Narrator:	And so Jack picked vegetables from the farmer's garden all day long in the hot sun. To pay him, the farmer gave him a big round of soft cheese.
Farmer:	Here is some cheese for all your work.
Jack:	Thank you.

Lazy Jack *(cont.)*

Narrator:	Good son that he was, Jack followed his mother's advice and put the cheese on his head. Unfortunately, the walk home was long and the sun was hot. The soft cheese melted along the way and ran down Jack's back. Jack knew he was in trouble.
Mother:	Do you have money?
Jack:	No. But I have cheese.
Mother:	Well, where is the cheese?
Jack:	It melted in the hot sun.
Mother:	You should have carried it in your hands.
Jack:	You are right. Next time, I will do that.
Narrator:	When morning came, Jack went back to the farmer.
Farmer:	I do have work for you.
Jack:	Good.
Narrator:	Jack worked all day baking bread for the farmer and his large family.
Farmer:	Here is a kitten for all your work.
Jack:	Thank you.
Narrator:	Like a good son, Jack carried the kitten in his hands. But the kitten didn't want to go with Jack and it didn't like the way Jack carried it. So it clawed Jack until he let it go. More trouble for Jack awaited.
Mother:	Do you have money?
Jack:	No. But I have a kitten.
Mother:	Well, where is the kitten?
Jack:	It scratched me, so I let it go.
Mother:	You should have put a string around it and pulled it behind you.
Jack:	You are right. Next time, I will do that.
Narrator:	The next day, Jack was lucky. The farmer had more work for him.
Farmer:	I do have work for you.
Jack:	Good.

Lazy Jack *(cont.)*

Narrator:	And Jack worked hard all day butchering and curing the farmer's meat.
Farmer:	Here is some meat for all your hard work.
Jack:	Thank you.
Narrator:	As he'd been told, Jack pulled a string from his pocket and tied it around the piece of meat. He dragged it down the road after himself. When he was almost home, Jack noticed the meat had become filthy. He knew he was in trouble again.
Mother:	Do you have money?
Jack:	No. But I have some meat.
Mother:	Well, where is the meat?
Jack:	I dragged it down the road and now it is dirty.
Mother:	You should have carried it on your back.
Jack:	You are right. Next time, I will do that.
Narrator:	And soon Jack had his chance. Jack asked the farmer for more work.
Farmer:	I do have work for you.
Jack:	Good.
Narrator:	Jack worked very hard caring for the farmer's donkeys. The farmer gave Jack a wonderful surprise.
Farmer:	Here is a donkey for all your hard work.
Jack:	Thank you!
Narrator:	Jack heeded his mother's advice. He hauled the donkey up onto his back. He staggered down the road toward home. But the donkey got very heavy, so Jack took a short cut. The short cut went past a castle and in this castle lived a very sad princess.
Princess:	I am very sad.
King:	Yes, you are.
Princess:	What can I do?
King:	We will look for someone to make you laugh.

Lazy Jack *(cont.)*

Princess:	We will?
King:	Yes. If he can make you laugh, I will make him rich.
Princess:	Okay.
Narrator:	Just then, Jack came puffing by with the poor donkey on his back.
King:	What is that?
Princess:	Oh, look!
King:	What is he doing?
Princess:	That boy has a donkey on his back! Ha, ha, ha! That is very funny!
King:	You laughed!
Princess:	I did, didn't I?
King:	We have to catch that boy!
Narrator:	The king and the princess rushed from the castle and stopped Jack.
King:	You made my daughter laugh.
Jack:	I did?
King:	Yes. I will make you rich.
Jack:	You will?
King:	Yes, I will.
Princess:	I like you.
Jack:	And I like you, too.
King:	Well, then, you can marry her and be rich, too!
Jack:	I can?
Princess:	Yes!
Jack:	Okay.
Narrator:	And that is precisely what happened. Jack and the princess lived happily ever after. And so did Jack's mother, who always knew Jack would do the right thing when it really mattered.

The End

Lazy Jack *(cont.)*

Mini-Lessons and Activities

- **Folk Tale Structure**

  After reading Lazy Jack, work as a group to identify the following elements of folk tales: main character, supporting characters, setting, sequence of events, complication, and resolution.

  Record the information on a chart, overhead, or board. The chart can be used again the next time the class reads a folk tale to provide practice in learning more about story elements. It can also be used as a pre-writing activity.

- **Comprehension**

  Have the children choose one character from the play. Encourage them to think of what the character might say *after* the story. Have the children draw the character they chose and add some speech bubbles. Write in the character's thoughts.

- **Character Traits**

  Have the children choose a character from the play. Write details about the character on the chart if you wish to do a group activity, or on a copy if you wish this to become an individual activity.

I AM Jack.
I am:
I live:
I eat:
I have:
I like:
I hate:
I wish:

The children will enjoy sharing their work.

- **Word Study**

  In order for the students to complete this activity, they must have a basic understanding of what nouns and verbs are. If they do not have this knowledge, provide a short discussion of what these words are. Remind them that a noun is a person, place, thing, or animal. Verbs are action words.

  Provide the students with a copy of the following words from the story: boy, cheese, donkey, money, string, catch, do, laugh, spill, look, the, yes, me, for, and.

  The students may cut the words apart. Working in pairs or individually, direct the children to put all the nouns in one group, all the verbs in one group, and all the "other" words in a third group. The teacher needs to check for understanding.

Drakestail

A Story from France

Multicultural Story Summary

Drakestail loans the king some money. On the way to get it back, he meets some friends—Fox, Wasp, Ladder, and River. He carts them along to the palace in his wagon. When they arrive, the king refuses to pay back the money. Instead, the king thinks of ways to get rid of poor Drakestail. First, the king throws the duck into a vicious poultry yard. Friend Fox jumps in and eats the horrible birds. Then the king puts Drakestail into a well. Ladder steps in and helps his friend out. The king throws Drakestail into a hot oven. Friend River puts out the fire in the oven. Then the king sets his soldiers on Drakestail. Friend Wasp calls in his own army to sting the soldiers. The king runs away and Drakestail becomes king.

Setting

A pond is on one end of the stage and a castle at the other. There is a road between them.

Suggested Props

little red wagon, crown, throne

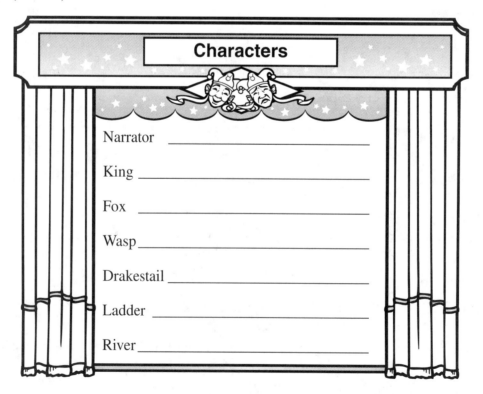

Characters

Narrator _____

King _____

Fox _____

Wasp _____

Drakestail _____

Ladder _____

River _____

Drakestail *(cont.)*

Word List

a	from	life	that
about	get	like	the
all	give	make	there
am	going	me	throne
an	good	men	tired
and	great	money	to
another	ha	morning	toss
are	has	must	very
ask	have	my	wagon
at	he	no	walk
back	help	not	want
be	here	of	wasp
borrowed	hey	oh	way
call	him	on	welcome
came	his	or	well
climb	hot	oven	what
come	hurry	ow	when
deep	I	pay	where
did	if	pull	who
do	in	quack	why
Drakestail	into	rid	will
Drakestail's	is	right	with
duck	it	river	work
end	king	see	would
find	king's	so	yes
for	knock	some	you
fox	know	stop	
friend	ladder	take	
friends	last	thank	

Drakestail

Narrator:	Once there was a very clever little duck named Drakestail. He lived in a country called France. As a duckling, he had been very poor. But as a grown-up duck, he had made a fortune. He kept his fortune in a little red wagon, which he pulled along behind himself. One day, the king heard about Drakestail's fortune.
King:	Well, well. So the duck has money! I must see him.
Narrator:	The king called Drakestail to the castle.
King:	Will you give me some money?
Drakestail:	Yes, I will.
King:	I will pay you back.
Drakestail:	That will be good.
Narrator:	So, the King took Drakestail's fortune. But the king did not pay Drakestail back, even though Drakestail was very patient about it.
Drakestail:	I am going to see the king. I will ask him about my money.
Narrator:	He got his little red wagon and set off for the castle, singing a little song.
Drakestail:	Quack, quack, quack, quack! When will I get my money back?
Narrator:	Soon he met his friend, the fox.
Fox:	Good morning, Drakestail.
Drakestail:	Good morning to you, Friend Fox.
Fox:	Where are you going?
Drakestail:	I am going to see the king.
Fox:	You are?
Drakestail:	Yes, I am.
Fox:	Why is that?
Drakestail:	He borrowed some money from me. I want it back.
Fox:	Will you take me with you?
Drakestail:	Yes, I will. I like to have my friends with me.
Fox:	That is right!
Drakestail:	If you walk all the way, Friend Fox, you will be tired. Climb into my wagon and I will pull you.
Fox:	Great!
Narrator:	So the fox jumped into Drakestail's wagon. They went on down the road. Drakestail sang his little song.
Drakestail:	Quack, quack, quack, quack! When will I get my money back?

Drakestail *(cont.)*

Narrator:	Before long, Drakestail saw his friend, the ladder, leaning against a wall.
Ladder:	Good morning, Drakestail!
Drakestail:	Good morning to you, Friend Ladder.
Ladder:	Where are you going?
Drakestail:	I am going to see the king.
Ladder:	You are?
Drakestail:	Yes, I am.
Ladder:	Why is that?
Drakestail:	He borrowed some money from me. I want it back.
Ladder:	Will you take me with you?
Drakestail:	Yes, I will. I like to have my friends with me.
Ladder:	That is right.
Drakestail:	If you walk all the way, Friend Ladder, you will be tired. Climb into my wagon and I will pull you.
Ladder:	Great!
Narrator:	The fox made room for the ladder in the little red wagon. They continued on down the road. Drakestail sang his little song.
Drakestail:	Quack, quack, quack, quack! When will I get my money back?
Narrator:	It wasn't long before Drakestail and his friends spied their friend River.
River:	Good morning, Drakestail.
Drakestail:	Good morning to you, Friend River.
River:	Where are you going?
Drakestail:	I am going to see the king.
River:	You are?
Drakestail:	Yes, I am.
River:	Why is that?
Drakestail:	He borrowed some money from me. I want it back.
River:	Will you take me with you?
Drakestail:	Yes, I will. I like to have my friends with me.
River:	That is right.
Drakestail:	If you walk all the way, Friend River, you will be tired. Climb into my wagon and I will pull you.
River:	Great!

       80

Drakestail *(cont.)*

Narrator:	So the fox and the ladder made room for the river in Drakestail's little red wagon. Off they went. Drakestail sang his little song.
Drakestail:	Quack, quack, quack, quack! When will I get my money back?
Narrator:	Soon they met their friend Wasp.
Wasp:	Good morning, Drakestail.
Drakestail:	Good morning to you, Friend Wasp.
Wasp:	Where are you going?
Drakestail:	I am going to see the king.
Wasp:	You are?
Drakestail:	Yes, I am.
Wasp:	Why is that?
Drakestail:	He borrowed some money from me. I want it back.
Wasp:	Will you take me with you?
Drakestail:	Yes, I will. I like to have my friends with me.
Wasp:	That is right.
Drakestail:	If you walk all the way, Friend Wasp, you will be tired. Climb into my wagon and I will pull you.
Wasp:	Great!
Narrator:	Although it was crowded in the little red wagon, friends always make room for more friends. They went on down the road. Drakestail sang his song.
Drakestail:	Quack, quack, quack, quack! When will I get my money back?
Narrator:	Soon they arrived at the castle. Drakestail went over the bridge and knocked on the door.
Drakestail:	Knock, knock, knock.
King:	Who is there?
Drakestail:	It is Drakestail.
King:	What do you want?
Drakestail:	I want my money back.
Narrator:	The King had other plans, however.
King:	Ha, ha, ha! He will NOT get his money back!
Drakestail:	Quack, quack, quack, quack! When will I get my money back?

Drakestail *(cont.)*

Narrator:	The King got very angry when he heard Drakestail's song. He sent out a soldier who pushed Drakestail into the poultry yard with all the other chickens and ducks.
Drakestail:	Quack, quack, quack, quack! When will I get my money back?
Narrator:	Of course, the very normal birds didn't understand anything Drakestail quacked. They just knew that something was very odd about him. They decided to peck at him.
Drakestail:	Hey! Stop that!
Narrator:	Drakestail had to think fast!
Drakestail:	Friend Fox! Friend Fox! Hurry, my friend, or Drakestail's life will be at an end!
Fox:	I will help you!
Narrator:	Friend Fox quickly jumped from the little red wagon and into the poultry yard. He ate the nasty, mean birds up and licked his lips with satisfaction.
Drakestail:	Thank you.
Fox:	You are very welcome.
Narrator:	And Drakestail began to sing again, a little louder this time.
Drakestail:	Quack, quack, quack, quack! When will I get my money back?
King:	Hey! That did not work. I will find another way to get rid of him!
Drakestail:	Oh, King! Where is my money?
King:	I know! I will toss him into a deep well!
Narrator:	The King sent for his soldiers and it was done.
Drakestail:	Hey! Stop that!
Narrator:	Poor Drakestail thought he'd never get out of the well. Then he began to think some more.
Drakestail:	Friend Ladder, Friend Ladder! Hurry, my friend, or Drakestail's life will be at an end!
Ladder:	I will help you!
Narrator:	The ladder stretched down into the well and helped Drakestail out.
Drakestail:	Thank you!
Ladder:	You are very welcome.
Narrator:	Feeling much better, Drakestail began to sing again. Loudly.

Drakestail *(cont.)*

Drakestail:	Quack, quack, quack, quack! When will I get my money back?
King:	That did not work. I will have to find another way to get rid of him.
Drakestail:	Oh, King! Where is my money?
King:	I will toss him into a hot oven! **Narrator:** The soldiers came and the deed was done.
Drakestail:	Hey! Stop that!
Narrator:	Poor, poor Drakestail! He was almost a cooked duck! But then he remembered his Friend River.
Drakestail:	Friend River, Friend River! Hurry, my friend, or Drakestail's life will be at an end!
River:	I will help you!
Narrator:	Whoosh! The river flooded the hot oven and Drakestail swam right out.
Drakestail:	Thank you!
River:	You are very welcome.
Narrator:	Drakestail was more determined than ever to get his money back from the king. At the top of his voice, he began to sing.
Drakestail:	Quack, quack, quack, quack! When will I get my money back?
King:	That did not work! I will have to find another way to get rid of him.
Drakestail:	Oh, King! Where is my money?
King:	I will call my men.
Narrator:	And so the King called in the soldiers. He hid them behind some curtains so they might spring out and capture the pesky duck once and for all.
King:	Come in, Drakestail.
Drakestail:	At last! I am here for my money.
King:	You will not get it.
Drakestail:	Hey!
Narrator:	At that very moment, the King motioned for his soldiers to come out from hiding and attack poor little Drakestail.
Drakestail:	Quack! Help!
Narrator:	The soldiers chased Drakestail around and around. Finally, Drakestail began to use his head instead of his feet.
Drakestail:	Friend Wasp, Friend Wasp! Hurry, my friend, or Drakestail's life will be at an end!

Drakestail *(cont.)*

Wasp:	I will help you!
Narrator:	The wasp came with his own very own army of wasps! They went after the King and his soldiers with their stingers.
King:	Ow! Ow!
Narrator:	The king and all the king's men ran from the castle as fast as they could. They ran far, far away.
Drakestail:	Quack! I came to get my money back.
Narrator:	He searched high and low. No money. He looked here and there. No money. He looked upstairs and downstairs. But there was no money.
Drakestail:	No money.
Narrator:	He sighed and sat down in the nearest chair, for he was very tired.
Fox:	You are on the king's throne.
Drakestail:	So I am.
Fox:	You would make a good king.
Drakestail:	I would?
Fox:	Yes, you would.
Narrator:	So it was that Drakestail became king. He saved the people of the kingdom lots and lots of money. And he and his friends lived happily ever after.

The End

Drakestail (cont.)

Mini-Lessons and Activities

- **Character Diary**

Have the students talk about what it would be like to be Drakestail or another character in the folk tale. On the overhead or on chart paper, model a diary entry for or with the children (depending on their proficiency with writing). Then have the children write about one of the things that happened to Drakestail in the story.

> *Monday*
> *I went to see the king at the castle. He said he needed some gold, so I gave some to him. I know he will give it back to me.*

- **Comprehension**

Have the children work together to design a map of Drakestail's world. Then have them place little footprints on the map to show where Drakestail traveled. Possible locales to include in the map might be: Drakestail's house, the castle, the fox's lair, the ladder leaning against a wall, the river, the wasps' next, the poultry yard, the well, the hot oven inside the castle, the soldiers' hiding place in the castle, the throne. Narrow this list down for younger children.

- **Learning about Fluency, Phrasing, and Expression**

The best way to help children begin to understand about good oral reading is through modeling reading behaviors. Good readers use their voices to show meaning by using appropriate expression and reading with correct phrasing and fluency. Select sentences from the text to use as an oral illustration for fluent reading, such as:

"Quack, quack, quack, quack!
When will I get my money back?"
"I am going to see the king."
"Hey! Stop that!"

Print the sentences on story strips, on the overhead, or on the board. Then read the sentences for the children. Have the children read the sentences with you. Be sure to emphasize correct expression, phrasing, and fluency. Volunteers might read the sentences aloud for the class.

For further work, the teacher can write the sentences on sentence strips. Cut the sentences into natural phrases. Practice reading the groups of words aloud with the children. Remind the children that good readers read in chunks or big pieces and not in single units or letter by letter.

The Mouse's Three Children

A Story from Tibet

Multicultural Story Summary

Mother Mouse has three remarkable children—a tiger, a peacock, and a boy. One day, the king's barber learns that the boy has untold riches—just from his hair and nail clippings. He runs to tell the king, who plots to have the best of the boy. He sets difficult tasks for the boy to accomplish. First, the boy must bring him four tigers. With the help of his brother tiger, the boy does this. Then the king asks for four peacocks. Brother peacock helps out. The greedy king tells the boy his mother, the little mouse, must fight his elephant. Knowing that the elephant has poor eyesight, the little mouse terrifies the fighting elephant by scampering all over his feet. The king has no choice but to declare the boy and his mother mouse winners. And so with his family's help, the boy wins the kingdom.

Setting

There is a mouse nest on one end of the stage and a palace on the other. Between them is a jungle.

Suggested Props

bit of tiger "fur," peacock feathers, jewels, crown, string

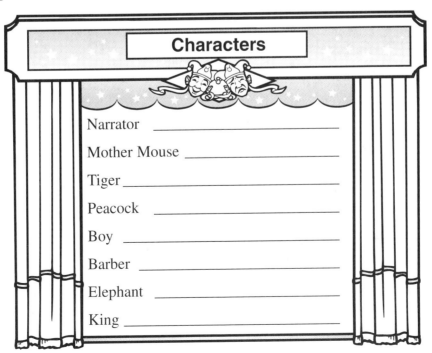

Characters

Narrator _____

Mother Mouse _____

Tiger _____

Peacock _____

Boy _____

Barber _____

Elephant _____

King _____

The Mouse's Three Children *(cont.)*

Word List

a	good	mouse	take
about	grrr	must	tell
air	ha	my	thank
all	hair	nails	that
am	have	name	the
and	hello	need	then
are	help	no	there
baby	here	not	this
be	hey	now	three
believe	him	off	tie
big	his	oh	tiger
boy	house	okay	tigers
bring	hundred	on	times
brother	I	only	to
brother's	if	or	too
but	in	other	toss
call	into	peacock	trouble
can	is	peacocks	turned
cut	it	pick	up
do	jewels	plan	want
down	jungle	problem	was
elephant	just	roof	watch
feather	king	said	we
feathers	know	see	well
fight	leave	she	went
for	left	sit	where
found	let's	slaves	why
four	little	so	will
fur	long	something	with
gates	loses	soon	won
get	me	stay	yes
give	mine	string	you
go	mother	tail	your

The Mouse's Three Children

Narrator:	Once upon a time, in a country called Tibet, a little mouse lived near the king's palace. Mother Mouse knew that when her children were grown they would be remarkable characters, indeed. She vowed that all her family would help each other whenever they needed each other. So when the mother mouse's first child was about to be born, she asked that it be strong. And it was—it was a tiger!
Mother:	Hey! You are not a mouse baby!
Tiger:	No, I am a tiger.
Mother:	You can not stay in my little house for long.
Tiger:	I know that.
Mother:	Soon you will be too big.
Tiger:	Yes. Then I will go to the jungle to be with the other tigers. You will?
Tiger:	Yes, I will. Here. Take this fur.
Mother:	Okay. Thank you.
Tiger:	If you need me, go to the jungle.
Mother:	Okay. I can do that.
Tiger:	Toss this fur into the air.
Mother:	Okay. I can do that.
Tiger:	Call my name three times.
Mother:	Okay. I will do that.
Narrator:	And when the tiger grew up, he left his mother with the promised handful of fur and went into the jungle. When Mother Mouse's second child was about to be born, she asked that it be beautiful. And it was—it was a peacock!
Mother:	Hey! You are not a mouse baby!
Peacock:	No. I am a peacock.
Mother:	You can not stay in my little house for long.
Peacock:	I know that.

The Mouse's Three Children (*cont.*)

Mother:	Soon you will be too big.
Peacock:	Yes. Then I will go to the jungle to be with the other peacocks.
Mother:	You will?
Peacock:	Yes, I will. Here. Take this feather.
Mother:	Okay. Thank you.
Peacock:	If you need me, go to the jungle.
Mother:	Okay. I can do that.
Peacock:	Toss this feather into the air.
Mother:	Okay. I can do that.
Peacock:	Call my name three times.
Mother:	Okay. I will do that.
Narrator:	When the peacock grew up, he left his mother just as he'd said. He gave her some peacock feathers and flew off into the forest. Soon, Mother Mouse was about to have her third child. She asked that it be wise, wealthy, and powerful. This child was a little boy.
Mother:	Hey! You are not a mouse baby! You are a boy!
Boy:	Yes, I am.
Mother:	But you will leave me.
Boy:	What?
Mother:	Your brother tiger and your brother peacock left me.
Boy:	But I will not leave you.
Mother:	Your brother tiger went into the jungle.
Boy:	I will not go into the jungle.
Mother:	Your brother peacock went into the jungle.
Boy:	I will not go into the jungle, Mother.
Mother:	Good.

The Script

The Mouse's Three Children *(cont.)*

Narrator:	So the boy grew. He stayed safe near the mouse family's home. One day, though, the king's barber happened to pass by the boy as he was walking to the palace. Since that was a barber's job, he noticed that the boy needed some grooming on his hair and nails.
Boy:	Hello.
Barber:	Hello there. Can I cut your hair?
Boy:	Okay.
Narrator:	Much to the barber astonishment, the hair he cut from the boy's head turned into precious gems as it fell to the ground.
Barber:	Oh, my! Can I cut your nails?
Boy:	Okay.
Narrator:	The nail clippings turned to beautiful turquoise stones as they fell to the ground.
Barber:	Oh, my! I must tell the king about this!
Boy:	What?
Narrator:	But the barber didn't answer the boy. He gathered up a handful of the jewels and ran straight to the king's palace.
Barber:	You will not believe this!
King:	What?
Barber:	I found a boy.
King:	So?
Barber:	When I cut his hair, the hair turned into jewels!
King:	Oh, yes?
Barber:	And when I cut his nails, the nails turned into jewels, too!
King:	Bring the boy to me.
Narrator:	The barber opened his hands and showed the jewels to the king. And then he went out to find the boy. He brought the boy back to the palace.
King:	You were in my jungle.

The Mouse's Three Children *(cont.)*

Boy:	Yes, I was.
King:	That is not good.
Boy:	Why not?
King:	The jungle is mine. Now you must give me something.
Boy:	What?
King:	You will give me four big tigers to watch my gates.
Boy:	Four big tigers?
King:	Yes—or you will be in trouble.
Boy:	Oh, no!
Narrator:	The boy ran home to his mother. He was crying.
Mother:	What is it?
Boy:	The king said I have to give him four big tigers to watch his gates.
Mother:	That is not a problem. See this fur?
Boy:	Yes.
Mother:	It is your brother's fur.
Boy:	Okay.
Mother:	Take it into the jungle.
Boy:	Okay, I will.
Mother:	Toss it into the air.
Boy:	Okay. I can do that.
Mother:	Call his name three times.
Boy:	I will do that. Thank you, Mother.
Narrator:	The boy did as his mother told him. He tossed the tiger fur into the air.
Boy:	Brother Tiger! Brother Tiger! Brother Tiger!
Tiger:	Grrrr! Here I am. What do you want, little brother?
Boy:	The king said I must give him four big tigers to watch his gates or I will be in trouble.
Tiger:	Ha! Is that all? I can get you a hundred tigers!

The Mouse's Three Children *(cont.)*

Boy:	But I only need four tigers.
Narrator:	The tiger opened his enormous mouth and let out a terrifying roar. Soon the whole jungle was full of tigers! The boy chose four of them and together they walked back to the palace.
Boy:	Here I am.
King:	I see you, boy.
Boy:	Here are your tigers.
King:	Well, good. Thank you.
Narrator:	Unfortunately, the king was greedy. He wanted more.
King:	Boy?
Boy:	Yes?
King:	You will give me four peacocks to sit on my roof.
Boy:	Four peacocks?
King:	Yes—or you will be in trouble.
Boy:	Oh, no!
Narrator:	Again, the boy ran home to Mother Mouse. He was very upset.
Mother:	What is it?
Boy:	The king said I have to give him four peacocks to sit on the roof.
Mother:	That is not a problem. See this feather?
Boy:	Yes.
Mother:	This is your brother's feather.
Boy:	Okay.
Mother:	Take it into the jungle.
Boy:	Okay. I will.
Mother:	Toss it into the air.
Boy:	Okay. I can do that.
Mother:	Call his name three times.
Boy:	I will do that. Thank you, Mother.

The Mouse's Three Children *(cont.)*

Narrator:	The boy followed his mother's directions. He tossed the peacock feathers into the air.
Boy:	Brother Peacock! Brother Peacock! Brother Peacock!
Peacock:	Here I am. What do you want, little brother?
Boy:	The king said I must give him four peacocks to sit on the roof or I will be in trouble.
Peacock:	Ha! Is that all? I can get you a hundred peacocks!
Boy:	But I only need four peacocks.
Narrator:	The peacock opened his beak and a piercing peacock call rang throughout the forest. At once, the air was filled with beautiful peacocks! The boy chose four of them. Together, they made their way to the palace.
Boy:	Here I am!
King:	I see!
Boy:	Here are your peacocks.
King:	Well, good. Thank you.
Narrator:	It was bad luck, indeed, that the king was still not satisfied. He cooked up an even-more-evil plan.
King:	Boy!
Boy:	Yes.
King:	Your mother will fight my elephant.
Boy:	But my mother is just a little mouse!
King:	Ha, ha! If she loses, you will be my slaves!
Boy:	Oh, no!
Narrator:	So the boy ran home with the bad news.
Boy:	What will we do?
Mother:	We will go to the king. It will be okay. I have a plan.
Boy:	You do?
Mother:	Oh, yes!
Boy:	What is the plan?

The Mouse's Three Children *(cont.)*

Mother:	Tie a string to my tail.
Boy:	Okay.
Mother:	Then pick me up.
Boy:	Okay, Mother.
Mother:	Let's go see the king.
Boy:	Here we go.
Narrator:	The boy did just as his mother asked. He tied on the string, picked her up, and carried her to the palace. The king was waiting for them with his fighting elephant.
King:	There you are, boy!
Boy:	Yes, we are here.
King:	Is that your mother?
Boy:	Yes, she is.
King:	If she loses, you will be my slaves.
Boy:	Okay.
Narrator:	So the king let the fighting elephant go. The boy put his little mother mouse on the ground.
Elephant:	I will get you!
Mother:	Oh, no! You will not!
Elephant:	Where are you?
Mother:	I am down here.
Elephant:	Where?
Mother:	Here!
Elephant:	What are you?
Mother:	I am a mouse.
Elephant:	But I can not see you!
Mother:	I know that! Ha, ha!

The Mouse's Three Children *(cont.)*

Narrator:	Mother Mouse jumped up on the big elephant's foot.
Elephant:	Hey! What is that?
Narrator:	He shook his enormous foot, but Mother Mouse held on.
Elephant:	Hey! Get off me!
Mother:	I will not get off!
Narrator:	And she didn't, either. The little mouse ran all over the elephant, who really couldn't see what was on his body. It drove him crazy!
Elephant:	Help! Help!
Mother:	Now I have you!
Narrator:	Indeed, the elephant couldn't take any more. He galloped off for the hills. The boy pulled the string and saved Mother Mouse from being carried away by the frightened fighting elephant.
Mother:	There!
Boy:	We won!
King:	Yes, yes. I see that you won, boy.
Boy:	And we can go.
King:	Yes, yes. You can go.
Narrator:	Soon after that, the boy—who was already wealthy—married the king's daughter. He became very powerful, just as his mother had hoped. He eventually even became a very good and wise king. The little mother mouse came to live in the palace. She was very proud of her three remarkable children—the tiger, the peacock, and the boy. They all lived happily ever after.

The End

The Mouse's Three Children *(cont.)*

Mini-Lessons and Activities

- **Fairy Tales vs. Folk Tales**

  There are a few basis differences between a fairy tale and a folk tale. Instruct the children in a few of these differences by reading stories from each sub-genre. After reading, lead the children to discuss some of the differences. Write these on an overhead transparency or on chart paper.

  Examples of well-know fairy tales might include: Snow White, Rumpelstiltskin, Cinderella, or Sleeping Beauty.

  Well-known folk tales might include: Clever Jack, Anansi stories, or Baba Yaga.

  Fairy tales often include magic, repetitive refrains (Fee Fi Fo Fum), magical folks, the supernatural, and are written with more details.

  Folk tales involve ordinary people, animals, and the use of quick wits.

  Have the children decide if The Mouse's Three Children is a fairy tale or a folk tale. Have them justify their choice.

- **Comprehension**

  Design a simple spinner. Use a paper plate as the spinner itself. Stick a brad through the center and hang a large paperclip on the brad to become the spinner. Divide the spinner into fourths. Label the fourths: characters, event or action, setting, character's feelings.

  Have the children spin. The teacher will ask questions of the children to demonstrate comprehension from that objective area. For example: if the child spins "setting," the teacher might ask: "Where does the folk tale begin?" or "Where does the tiger live?"

  Continue spinning until each child in the group has had a chance to spin and answer a question.

- **Character**

  Design a "Wanted" Poster for one of the characters in the play. This activity builds good descriptive writing skills.

WANTED

picture

Name:_____
Age: _____
Last Known Address: _____
Physical Description:_____
Special Features: _____
Other Information:_____

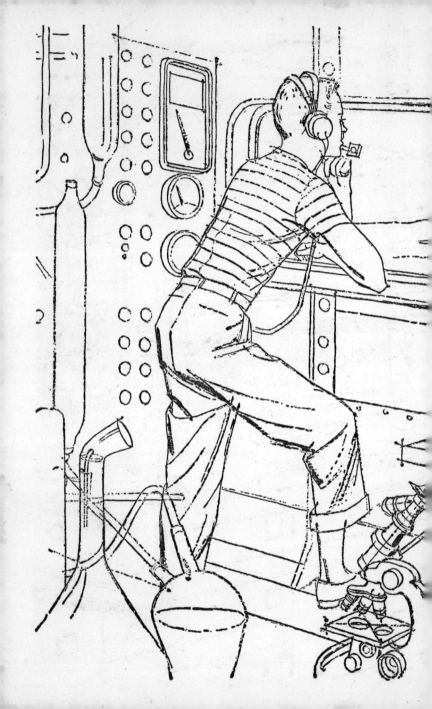